Roadmaps for Living

More Rules of the Road

By
Olivia M. Cloud

R.H. Boyd
Publishing
CORPORATION
A GLOBAL NAME IN PUBLISHING FOR OVER 100 YEARS

Nashville, Tennessee

I0157215

Roadmaps for Living
More Rules of the Road

Olivia M. Cloud

Scripture quotations marked NIV are taken from The Holy Bible, *New International Version*, © 1973, 1978, 1984 by the International Bible Society. Used by permission of Zondervan Publishing House. Scripture quotations marked KJV are taken from The Holy Bible, *King James Version*. Scripture quotations marked NLT are taken from The Holy Bible, *New Living Translation*, copyright © 1996 by Tyndale Charitable Trust. Used by permission of Tyndale House Publishers.

R.H. Boyd Publishing Corporation
6717 Centennial Boulevard
Nashville, Tennessee 37219

ISBN: 158942218-X

Printed in the United States of America

CONTENTS

"Thy word is a lamp unto my feet,
and a light unto my path."
Psalm 119:105 (KJV)

"Whatever you do, whether in word or deed, do it all
in the name of the Lord Jesus, giving thanks to God
the Father through Him."
Colossians 3:17 (NIV)

INTRODUCTION
Roadmaps for Living

THE DEMANDS of life can be quite overwhelming at times. Stress is taking a dreadful toll on our nation's health. Statistics tell us that more than 66 percent of physician visits to are related to the kind of stress that comes from being overwhelmed. Ours is a world that every year seems to get more complex, more massive, and more unmanageable. As we receive more information, invent more complex creations, and grapple with more unmanageable life issues, we have to make more choices.

Sometime in recent history, someone coined the phrase "information overload." With each passing year, we learn more and more about ourselves and about the world we live in. A deluge of new facts is upon us before we have the chance to assimilate the old facts. In this information age, instead of being more confident in our choices, we seem less certain than ever. Why? Because we have too much information.

Every day we learn more and more information related to the choices we must make, like whether our diets should be low in fat or low in carbohydrates. Every day we face choices. We face big choices, like whether to accept a position with another company or whether to marry a certain person. We make small choices daily, like whether to have fish or chicken for dinner.

Beyond the everyday choices, we all face circumstances that require us to call upon a higher authority. One of the most difficult struggles of the Christian life is receiving and accepting divine guidance to help us in making sound choices. Christians often speak with confidence about doors in life being opened or closed by God. Most Christians have experienced the feeling of being "led" to do something. These concepts of divine guidance, while subjective, are not contrary to Scripture. In the Bible, God often closed doors to His people or "led" His servants to places or into circumstances for his own purposes.

As Christians, we know that God has come to dwell in us. He works in us to make us new creatures and guides us from within. Every Christian has at some time felt that God wanted him or her to do something in particular, if it was no more than to repent and believe the Gospel. Therefore, it is fair to assert that experiencing the inner "leading" of the Spirit is common to believers.

Common to followers of Jesus Christ is learning that it is not always easy to distinguish the voice of God from those of the world, the flesh, and the devil. Many times when we start in a particular direction and meet with resistance or obstacles we deduce, "God closed that door to keep me from going through." But was it really God closing that door or do we sometimes confuse the obstacles we must overcome with a closed door? How quickly do we give up when things don't fall into place according to our timetable? What tells us to give up?

Facing obstacles that result from the choices we make is difficult. There is a common belief in our Western world of comfort and ease that struggle and obstacles have no place in our lives. Making choices can be quite a daunting process. Some people seem to think that they can avoid making decisions and just drift along with life. They make their decisions by not deciding. Their philosophy is like that of Timon and Pumbaa from the motion picture, "The Lion King"—hakuna matata — "no worries."

Taking a laissez faire attitude about decisions is in fact a decision to be unthinking about what happens to you in life. Making no choice means choosing to give in to the forces that are at work in the world for good or evil and letting them rule over you. Hakuna matata doesn't work in the real world. There's no such thing as having "no worries for the rest of your days." In fact it didn't even work for young Simba in the movie. Eventually, he decided to go back to his native den and assume leadership of the lions there.

God never promised that our paths would always be smooth and straight. We have been told to expect a measure of hardship. In fact, struggle is an essential part of the growth process for God's children as we learn to persevere and press on for the prize. There is no set formula or mathematical equation guaranteed to sort out solutions and answers for God's people. But inherent to the process of growth is learning to hear the "still small voice" of God above the storms of life and to recognize what is from God and what is not. The Word of God is given to us as an objective revelation of God's will. His Word is our roadmap for living. It protects us from hearing the wrong voices.

Chapter 12 in the Book of Hebrews discusses a "great cloud of witnesses" (v. 1). Through their lives and the lives of other faithful people of God, we can gain wisdom and direction for living, even in these modern times. Ecclesiastes 1:9 (NIV) reads, "What has been will be again, what has been done will be done again; there is nothing new under the sun." By divine design, the experiences of the ancients are equally relevant to us today. Times may have changed but God's roadmap to guide His people has not changed.

In Isaiah 48:17 (NIV), God says, "I am the LORD your God, who teaches you what is best for you, who directs you in the way you should go." The Good Shepherd stands before His sheep and leads them safely in His ways. In John 10, Jesus expounds on this guidance process. His sheep "will never follow a stranger; in fact, they will run from him because they do not recognize a stranger's voice" (v. 3, NIV). If we listen to His voice, when we are faced with choices, He will speak to us.

Learning God's voice requires a thorough knowledge of His will and purposes to help direct our actions and decisions. Christians live with the general acceptance that making our own decisions and ignoring God's way is not how we want to live. We accept Him and His way because He has accepted us, taking us into His friendship and His family. This means that when we are faced with a decision, we decide according to what is consistent with our God's Word.

Knowledge of God's will comes first and foremost from God's Word, which reveals His plan, principles, and purposes. This knowledge is essential to receiving divine guidance. For example, Abraham's knowledge of God's Word led him to move in the right direction in receiving God's guidance. Abraham took steps to find Isaac a wife so that God's plan was furthered through future generations.

Abraham knew his son must have a family in order for the covenant blessings to be received. Abraham understood this, so he didn't sit idly and wait for God's plan to be fulfilled. He takes appropriate action which, in this case, meant finding for a wife for Isaac.

Some people seem to think that receiving God's guidance means doing nothing. They sit down, both physically and spiritually, because they are waiting for God to provide. God wants us to do our part, but He wants us to do it while being guided by the knowledge of His Word. Abraham didn't have a specific commandment from God's Word, but he had enough information to apply biblical principles to the situation. Many times we don't have a specific command from the Bible but we can still apply principles from God's Word and be assured of being in His will. Through God's guidance we can make wise decisions by applying biblical principles regarding such issues as purity, righteousness, and so forth.

No matter what choices, decisions, or obstacles we face, God's people should trust and receive only the Word of God for guidance. As a lamp to our feet and a light to our path (Psalm 119:105), His Word gives illumination to our dark world, empowering us to make righteous choices.

Psalm 1 compares the person who meditates on God's Word to a bountiful tree planted by streams of water where it never dries up and always bears fruit. If we submit ourselves to the guidance of God, then we must build our lives on the Word of God. We must read it, study it, meditate upon it, and then apply it to our lives. Jesus indicated that we do not live by bread (material elements) alone but by the Word of God (Matthew 4:4).

As we are prayerfully reading the Word of God, often the Holy Spirit will speak to us, illuminating our minds and helping us to apply the Word to our specific situation. God does not want His people to be lost. Therefore, in giving us Roadmaps for Living, He causes His Word to speak and bring consolation and confirmation to us through the Holy Spirit. Divine guidance through His Word is not simply some ethereal or subjective experience but rather a witness by the Spirit that harmonizes with the revealed Word of God.

The apostle Paul admonishes in Colossians 3:17 (NIV) "Whatever you do, whether in word or in deed, do it all in the name of the Lord Jesus, giving thanks to God the Father through him." With every word we utter and every deed we accomplish, we do as earthly representatives of God. When we have choices to make, let us make those choices that represent Him the best. We should be mindful to make choices for which we can give Him thanks. We cannot go wrong when we establish God's roadmap for our guiding principles.

CHAPTER ONE
Praise God for Everything!

— PSALM 104:24-35 —

THE BEGINNING verse in this passage is a transitional verse. In the previous 23 verses of the psalm, the psalmist has, in great detail, described the wonders of God's creative handiwork. If the psalmist were here today, he would be singing, "Our God is an awesome God. He reigns from heaven above."

It has been speculated that the psalmist perhaps had an experience that caused him to pause and consider the greatness of God. It's an awesome thing to reflect on the greatness of God. How often do we stop and really think about the power and majesty of God?

Most of us go about our days experiencing God's blessings without really thinking about how good God is. In summer, we complain about how hot it is. During the winter months, we complain about the cold temperatures and the snow. When it's dry, we pray for rain. When it starts to rain, we complain about the wet and dreary weather. But in the midst of all our complaining, do we consider the handiwork of the God who set all of this into motion? The writer of Psalm 104 certainly did. In verse 24, after he has considered all of the things God has done, he says, "How many are your works, O LORD! In wisdom you made them all; the earth is full of your creatures" (NIV) His statement reflects both what has been done and what is yet to come.

It is as if he has been overwhelmed by the awesomeness of God and has burst forth into a song of praise. His praise song reveals a great deal about the magnificent, multifaceted, and incomprehensible nature of the God whom we serve.

GOD'S POSSESSIONS

We do not serve a poor God. The earth, the psalmist says, is full of God's possessions. Anyone can understand the concept of a person whose house is filled with his or her possessions. We should think of the earth as God's house, and everything in it belongs to Him. If we were to think of God like a designer, like Gucci® or Versace®, everything would have God's trademark logo on it. If humankind truly treated the earth like it belongs to God and not to us, we would give every endeavor to preserving the precious earth that bears God's logo just as we diligently preserve our clothing, purses, shoes, and cars that bear prestigious labels. We recognize clothing designed by FUBU® or Phat Farm®, or handbags by Gucci®, Fendi®, or Louis Vuitton®. We recognize the symbol of Mercedes®, BMW®, and Lexus® automobiles, and we view all of these things as marks of quality. God made us all and our lives should reflect His mark of excellence. Or as the kids' T-shirt used to say, "I know I'm somebody 'cause God don't make no junk!"

The psalmist has considered everything that God has made on earth and deemed it to be of the most amazing quality. He reflects on the sea—water. He is awed by God's creation of water and all that it does. Water quenches our thirst and provides nourishment for vegetation. And that same water can carry ships from one place to another. The waters were home to the great sea creature, the Leviathan, which may have been a giant whale, and some have suggested it may even have been a dinosaur.

Whatever the Leviathan's identity, so great and awesome is God that the mighty creatures of the sea-creatures that are capable of bringing certain death and destruction to human beings-get all that they receive from the Creator. As great as such creatures are, the psalmist recognizes that there is something even greater. The psalmist is giving praise to that something greater, which is the creator God. By his written testimony here, the psalmist understands the power of the Creator God. That means he understands true power. God had proven, and continues to prove His power throughout history. He has proven His power to speak the universe into creation and bring order to it by His word. He has proven His power to speak victory into the hearts of fearful soldiers. He has proven His power to speak healing into sick bodies. By His word He has caused flesh, life, and spirit to come upon dead bones. By His word He has made the winds and seas cease their troubling. His power does not come and go. God has always been all-powerful, and He always will be.

GOD'S POWER

As he reflects on God's power, in verses 27-29, the psalmist is saying, "God, you are so great that even these great sea creatures [perhaps the largest creature that they knew in that day] look to you for food at the right time." As mighty and fearful as they were, their sustenance came at God's hand. And should God hide from them (v. 29), they would be terrified. When God takes away their breath, they die and return to dust. And so it is with every creature that God has made.

A man of rather large and imposing stature once shared how he learned an important life lesson about his own vulnerability. Because of his size, the man had grown to think of himself as powerful. No bully ever tried to kick sand in his face at the beach or pick a fight with him. His stride held confidence and power. But one day he was walking down the street eating a muffin for breakfast and a tiny bit of it became lodged in his windpipe. The man nearly choked to death right on the street! The experience was frightening, but it helped him to recognize the fragility of all human life, and his own in particular. Before that day he had feared nothing, but one that day he realized that despite his commanding presence, something as tiny as a crumb of bread could have taken his life in a moment. That fateful day, on a New York street corner, a 6'5", 300-lb. man came to recognize that there is indeed a Power greater than himself, One who held authority over his life.

If you have ever had a near-death experience, you know that there is somebody else in control of your life-and that the only reason you are still breathing is because He's got a reason for keeping you alive. God provides every breath that we take. And when He decides to take it away, we are no more. That's true power!

The psalmist's understanding of God's power is comparable to the centurion's appreciation for the power and authority of His Son in Matthew 8. It has been observed that truly great leaders respect the power and authority of other leaders. The centurion sent for Jesus to heal his ailing servant, although he was a man of great authority, he did not consider himself worthy to have Jesus enter his home. Instead, the officer had great confidence that if Jesus would simply speak the word, his servant would get well. As he explained in verse nine: "For I myself am a man under authority, with soldiers under me. I tell this one, 'Go,' and he goes; and that one, 'Come,' and he comes. I say to my servant, 'Do this,' and he does it." (NIV) Because he was a man who had power, he understood how it may be used. He had faith in Jesus and knew the immense power that Jesus possessed and would make available for His servant.

Like the centurion, the psalmist knows that all the Creator has to do is say the word and life comes to some and death to others. This is the God we want on our side. The psalmist understood that we should be fearful should God ever turn away. Oh, help us if He should ever turn His face from us!

And while we believe that our God would never turn away from us, certain life experiences can cause us to feel like He has abandoned us. A group of people had a meeting and began to discuss the merits of Fannie Crosby's hymn, "Pass Me Not" (O Gentle Savior). Some in the group deemed the song irrelevant and theologically unsound. As the group continued to debate the merits of the song, a pastor of longstanding interjected. He said that while it may not be theologically sound to assert that God will pass by or turn away from those who call Him Father, sometimes the circumstances of life can cause us to wonder if God has indeed turned His face away from us. Thus we sing and cry out, "While on others Thou art calling, do not pass me by."

In life we learn that many of our beliefs that are not deemed theologically sound are certainly beneficial and true. For example, some people don't believe that the Lord moves in mysterious ways. But then He blesses you to live long enough to witness the impossible and illogical. Or you gain a station in life when all of the odds are against you. That's when you know that the Lord moves in mysterious ways!

Because God is so powerful and capable of doing so much for us, we do not want Him to ever turn away from us. The psalmist affirms what a horrible thing this is to experience. We know that God does not turn His back; however, in life we will endure experiences that cause us to believe that He has done so. Even Jesus cried out, "My God, why have you forsaken me?" All of us may have wondered "God, where are You?" at some time or another. And then we recognize, as the song "(You Can't Hurry God) He's Right on Time" says, "He may not come when you want Him but He's right on time."

Our experiences with the Lord and our maturation in the faith teach us to believe in the impossible—like God sending down fire from the sky—because the God we serve sits high and looks low. He is the God of the downtrodden and oppressed. He is the God who moves in mysterious ways and makes the impossible possible. Indeed, it is for all of these reasons and more that the psalmist writes that we should praise God—for His goodness, His power, and His providence—recognizing that it would be a terrible thing if He decided to hide His face from His people.

GOD'S PURPOSES

In verse 31 the psalmist begins a succession of praise to God for His creative work. He blesses God for His creative wisdom. He recognizes that God made us for a purpose. "May the Lord rejoice in his works . . ." When we are considering His creative handiwork, we should think about why God created human beings. If we devote ourselves to the calling He has for us, He will rejoice in the fact that He has made us. If God creates someone to write, work to produce Christian education resources, and preach the Gospel, then that is what that believer must do and devote his or her best to it because the Lord should always be able to rejoice that He made each and every human being. We should want Him to look at our faithfulness and be pleased because we are fulfilling the purpose for which He made us.

The prophet says of God in chapter 49 of the Book of Isaiah, "he who formed me in the womb to be his servant." How often do we stop to consider what God created us to do and rejoice in the fact that He created us for a purpose? That we are able to do what He made us to do and, therefore, we are pleasing Him? When God called the prophet Jeremiah, He said, "Before I formed you in the womb I knew you, before you were born I set you apart; I appointed you as a prophet to the nations" (Jer. 1:5, NIV). Jeremiah tried to find excuses not be a prophet. But God basically said "No, I created you for this purpose."

Moses tried to find excuses not to be the chosen deliverer of his people. But God said to him, "No, I created you for this purpose." For at least ten years I tried to find excuses to keep from being a minister of the Gospel—a preacher. But God would not turn me loose. He needed me to become willing to do what He wanted. My father, who served in ministry for seventy-two years, often counseled young people who were wondering whether God was calling them into ministry. Generally, they were surprised at his response, which was, "Well, if you can help it, don't do it!" His reasoning was that if the person could help it, God really had not called him or her.

Has God ever gotten hold of you because He had something for you to do? How often do you consider the fact that God has created you for a purpose? Furthermore, do you know what that purpose is and are you earnestly living in fulfillment of that purpose? Some people don't know what they're doing here, but you can always identify a man or woman who knows that he or she was created for a purpose.

Some people may look at that person and turn up their noses saying, "Humph, she thinks she's special." When I've had those painful experiences, my response generally is, "Well, yes, I do think I'm special because I know that God has created me for a purpose. I know that God knows my name and He picked me to do a special thing for Him. I have a reason for being on this earth. I know that I'm not here by accident! That makes me somebody special!"

It shouldn't matter if the president of the United States knows your name; the president is powerful but was not your creator. Don't worry if Oprah and Larry King don't know your name. Oprah can't give you purpose in life and Larry King does not control when you take your last breath. Don't be concerned if no one ever calls you to be interviewed on the Tom Joyner Morning Show, because they don't know your name.

The reason none of us should care about the world knowing who we are is because the God who created the heavens and the earth, who created the sun, moon, and stars and set them into place, and who can stop their action by His word—the God who breathed the breath of life into every living thing—knows every person's name! That makes every person somebody!

He has made us all "somebody" and without Him we are nothing! Our sense of significance is not determined by our clothes, our car, our house, or our job—a person may never receive all these things and still be somebody. So that means we need to praise God and never stop because in His eyes we're always somebody. That's what the psalmist decided to do:" I will sing to the Lord as long as I live. I will sing praise to my God while I have my being" (v. 33, KJV). It reminds me of a song that I often heard growing up in church, "I believe I'll serve the Lord, while I have the chance."

▲ We've got to praise Him and serve Him while we have the chance because everything we have, including the air we breathe, belongs to Him.

▲ We've got to praise Him because everything that we are has come because of His goodness.

▲ We've got to praise Him because He holds all possessions on this earth.

▲ We've got to praise Him because He holds all power.

▲ We've got to praise Him because He alone is capable of giving true purpose to life.

Finally, the psalmist adds a petition to "let the sinners be consumed . . . and the wicked be no more" (v. 35, KJV). In other words, he is asking that be moved out of the way, those who are intent on stopping God's children from doing what He has called them to do. Sometimes we have trouble with this notion of asking God to let the wicked be gone or to get rid of certain folk. But when you know that God has created you for a purpose, and somebody is trying to hinder you from doing the work of the Lord, you fully understand that they need to be gone—and they will be gone! In 1 Chronicles 16:22 God says, "Touch not mine anointed, and do my prophets no harm." Anyone trying to do harm to God's people had better leave them alone. It's not a good thing to pursue the destruction of those God has chosen for a purpose.

Knowing that God has a purpose for us will move us to pray for whatever we need to do His will. Because doing what God wants is the only way we can find true fulfillment.

Is your life feeling empty? Do you want meaning and purpose in life? Start praising God now and don't stop. Whether you are sure of your purpose or not, or even you have evildoers trying to hinder you from fulfilling His plans, praise God through all things. If you stop praising Him, you may start to forget all that He has done, all that He has set in motion so that you may be used to do His will. When we praise Him for all things continuously, we are inextricably drawn to the reality that He is the God of all power and that He has a special purpose for us.

PRAISE GOD FOR EVERYTHING!
Questions

1. Do you make it a practice to reflect with thanksgiving on the wonders of God's creation? What aspect of God's creative work are you most grateful for?

2. How have you, through your behavior, shown disrespect for what God has created?

3. Have you ever had an experience that reminded you of your own human fragility and vulnerability? If so, how did it affect your understanding or perception of the Most High God?

4. Both the psalmist who authored Psalm 104 and the centurion of Matthew 8 understood the sovereign rule and authority of God over all things. Have you accepted God's authority in your own life? In what ways has God made you aware of His authority over all things?

5. Have you ever wondered, "God, where are you?" during a difficult time of your life? How did God affirm His presence and authority in your life even though it seemed, for a time, that God was not there?

6. Write a letter to God, thanking Him for being the Creator of all things, and more specifically, for being the Creator of you.

7. Do you believe it's acceptable for God's people to believe they are special? In what ways has God revealed to you that you are a special creation?

8. How has God demonstrated to you that He is aware of your presence in the world and that He knows your name?

9. How can you help fellow Christians with low self-esteem have a healthy identity as special creations of God? What Scripture passages would you share with them to show them that every human being is a special creation of God created with a purpose?

10. How can you help lead unbelievers to understand that God created them to be special and that they are special to Him? What Scripture passages would you share with them to show them that every human being is a special creation of God created with a purpose?

11. Why should you praise God for all things and during all times?

12. Are you hesitant to ask God to deal swiftly with those who attempt to carry out evil or do harm to God's people? Why do you think the psalmist was so forceful in his appeal to God to vanish sinners from the earth and to let sinners be no more?

CHAPTER TWO
Trust God Through Life's Storms

— MARK 6:45-52 —

THE GOSPELS record two specific incidents in which Jesus' twelve disciples were caught in a storm. The first encounter is one familiar to us—the storm suddenly appears while Jesus is asleep in the back of the boat. The disciples are terrified, but they manage to awaken Jesus. He calms the storm with the words we know so well, "Peace, be still." And the disciples were amazed that just by His word, this man could control the elements of nature.

But the disciples experienced a second storm. (Life is full of storms, isn't it?) The second experience had many similarities to the first—all twelve disciples were there, the storm was intense, the disciples were terrified and had to work frantically to stay afloat.

But there are some vast differences in the first and second storms. Unlike the first storm, during the second storm Jesus was not with the disciples when the storm hit. They could not run to Him to calm this second storm. In this second storm, no immediate command was given to the elements. But the most critical difference in this second storm are, first, the only reason they encountered this storm on the Sea of Galilee was because Jesus told them to get on the boat. They encountered a crisis because they obeyed Jesus. Surely He knew the storm was coming, but He told them to get on the boat anyway. It is easy to accept that Jesus knew the storm was coming, because if meteorologists, with all of their scientific training and instrumentation, can forecast a storm, surely God Incarnate could do the same.

The critical difference in this storm is—according to verse 48—that Jesus saw the disciples straining at the oars because the wind was against them. That means Jesus stood at the shore watching while His disciples struggled desperately to prevent the boat from capsizing. Many of the twelve disciples on board were experienced fishermen, so if they were struggling, it was a terrible storm.

Likewise, many of us are experienced Christians, but it doesn't mean that we won't have to struggle to get out of life's storms. Critical life events are an integral part of the Christian journey. We tell ourselves things like:

▲ "God never said every day would be sunshine."

▲ "He'll see you through."

▲ "He knows how much you can bear."

▲ "If He brings you to it, He'll bring you through it."

Still, the question begs asking: Why would God deliberately send His disciples into a storm and then watch them struggle through it? Remember, the only reason that the twelve were on the boat was because Jesus had told them to get on. Think about that. You're struggling in a life storm—but the only reason you're struggling in that place is because God sent you there! The only reason you're in a storm is because you obeyed God.

Think about the storms of your life. Can you imagine that Jesus knew they were coming and did nothing to prevent them? A lost job, the betrayal of a friend, infidelity in a marriage; the downfall of a child; the loss of a loved one; a devastating financial crisis—these kinds of storms are painful, but common in life.

It's bad enough to think about going through a storm, but what happens to your faith when you stop to realize that Jesus, the Good Shepherd, is standing by watching you go through your storm? How does it feel to think about the fact that He didn't try to stop you from walking into that storm. He didn't try to stop the storm, either. Furthermore, He didn't even try to warn you. He let you walk in. It may even feel like all Jesus did was stand by and watch as you struggled to get yourself out.

If we accept this as truth, then sometimes it's safe to say, "You're not paranoid, God really is setting you up." Normally, we believers don't like to think about it, but the reality is that God has indeed set up people of faith to go through some storms in life:

▲ God hardened Pharaoh's heart before sending Moses to demand that he let the Israelites go (Exodus 4:21).

▲ God hardened Pharaoh's heart after the Israelites had left Egypt and thought they were headed for the Promised Land (Exodus 14:4, 17).

▲ God told Abraham to sacrifice his son of promise, Isaac, on Mount Moriah (Genesis 22).

▲ The Lord sent an evil spirit upon Saul, which caused him to want to kill David (1 Samuel 16:14).

▲ God sent Elijah to the widow of Zarephath to ask for food when she was down to her last bite (1 Kings 17:10-15).

STRENGTH

There is a story about a man who had watched a butterfly struggle to work its way out of a cocoon. As he watched, he had sympathy for the young butterfly and thought that the struggle was too cruel to endure. So, he decided to help the next butterfly avoid that struggle. He cut the cocoon open, allowing the butterfly to simply fall out. But then the man discovered something terrible: the butterfly could not fly! Its wings were too weak and underdeveloped. What the man learned was that the struggle for release from the cocoon was actually good for the butterfly. The struggle makes the butterfly's wings stronger so that it can achieve flight.

In that same vein, could it be that by sending His disciples into the storm Jesus was preparing them for the time when His physical presence would not be with them? Think about it. Everything was in the boat with them but Jesus. There was fish, water, confusion, fear, and anxiety in the boat, but no Jesus. Where was Jesus? Time passed, and still there was no Jesus. Some Christians have been struggling in their personal storms for a long time, and have been praying and doing their best, and they wonder, "Where is Jesus?"

No matter how long you have been on your Christian walk, like all believers, you will experience storms. The disciples were experienced men of the sea, not neophytes, but they could not avoid the storm. They made their living on the sea. All of their combined years of experience didn't stop them from being stricken with fear and panic when the storm arose. So if these professional seamen were frightened, this was a serious storm. It was like nothing they had encountered before; and of all the times for them to be in a storm, Jesus was absent. He was nowhere to be found. During the first storm, He was in the boat with them. It's easy to go through a storm when we have the assurance that Jesus is with us. Sometimes we go through a terrible life storm, but all the while we are confident of God's presence with us, bringing us through and guiding us every step of the way. But there are other times, other storms, when we feel like He has abandoned us and the storms get even harder. During some life storms we feel like we are in them all alone. But, even when we cannot feel the strength of His presence, we can know that He is watching us, monitoring our movements. Jesus never stopped watching His disciples from the shoreline. It is always more important that God sees us than for us to see God.

Can you imagine God standing by watching us struggle like the man watched the butterfly come out of the cocoon? Perhaps it is tempting for God to reach down and swiftly extricate us from our struggle like that man did for the first butterfly; but in His divine wisdom He doesn't.

Sometimes we're angry with God because He won't help us get out of the storm. Our struggle with God reminds me of my friend Carol's struggle to recover her health. Carol has a powerful testimony about coming through an intense and lasting storm. Many years ago, Carol and her husband were in a terrible automobile accident. Carol was in a coma for months afterward. When she came out of her coma, she had trouble remembering how to do the simplest of functions, like how to tie her own shoes. Hers was a long rehabilitation period. To make matters worse, her husband determined he couldn't handle the pressure and filed for divorce. Carol moved in with her mother as she struggled to put her life back together. She recalled that during the early days of her recuperation, she would often slide off the couch, having poor muscle control. Not once did her mother help her get back on the couch. "I remember being so angry at her for not helping me," Carol confessed. She remembered that it sometimes would take her more than an hour to work her way back on the couch. And although Carol's body and life never fully recovered, she is able to live a full and functional life, in part because of her mother's determination to make her grow and develop in her own strength.

God knows when our storms are coming, but we don't. Jesus could have warned the Twelve about the impending storm. He could have cautioned them to stay behind until the storm was over. But He didn't do any of that. Why? Jesus will let His disciples go through a storm because, even though we don't like the struggle, we learn more about Him and grow closer to Him by going through storms than we do by living in sunshine. Our faith and dependency on Him are strengthened through the storms of life.

The disciples' experience is an important reminder to all believers that just because you are encountering a storm, it doesn't mean that you are outside of God's will. Too many Christians have adopted a form of pop theology that espouses, "If I'm a Christian and live on a certain spiritual plane, I will not experience any storms." But the reality is that all of us as believers are either in a storm, just coming out of a storm, or soon will be on our way into a storm.

The storms of life give you strength. How many storm experiences have actually helped you to triumph in a situation down the road?

- ▲ A storm you went through in your family?
- ▲ A storm you went through on your job?
- ▲ A storm you went through with your finances?
- ▲ A storm you went through with your spouse?
- ▲ A storm you went through with your health?

TESTIMONY

When we go through life's storms, at times it may feel like we're not going to make it. But it's the very experience with struggle that gives us a testimony. What good is a Christian without a testimony? Our testimony comes from the storms of life, not the easy rides. If you want to have a powerful Christian testimony, you have to go through some storms.

What kind of testimony would the disciples have had if the boat trip had been an easy ride? What kind of testimony would they have had if they could only say, "Well, we got on the boat and didn't have a bit of trouble"? What would their faith response be? If easy times were all Christians ever had to talk about, our testimonies would be rather dull and mundane. Through the experiences of life, we need to be able to say, as do the lyrics of Andre Crouch, "If I never had a problem, I wouldn't know that God could solve them. Through it all, I've learned to trust in Jesus."

What kind of testimony would Moses have had if he had gone to Pharaoh with, "God said, 'Let my people go,'" and Pharaoh responded "Okay"? But God hardened Pharaoh's heart first and then threw Moses into a storm. What kind of testimony would the Israelites have had if they had never been trapped between the Red Sea and Pharaoh's army? But God hardened Pharaoh's heart to go after them even after he had given them permission to leave (Exodus 14).

How much different our lives would be if God didn't allow us to run into a few storms! How different would your faith testimony be? How different would the testimonies of God's faithful throughout the Bible be?

▲ What if God hadn't allowed Sarah's womb to stay closed until she was in her nineties? (Genesis 21) She would not have understood the power of the God she served.

▲ What if God hadn't asked Abraham to sacrifice his son Isaac (Genesis 22)? It was through that experience on Mount Moriah that Abraham came to know God as Jehovah-jireh. For it was at the threshold of his storm that Abraham learned just how the Lord will provide. Through some of life's storms you learn just how the Lord will provide.

▲ What if God hadn't allowed Shadrach, Meshach, and Abednego to go into the furnace and through the fire before sending His Son to rescue them? (Daniel 3) God used these three faithful men to demonstrate His power to an entire nation.

▲ What if God hadn't allowed Daniel to go into the lion's den? (Daniel 6) Surely the experience altered his entire understanding of and relationship to God.

▲ What if the Lord hadn't sent an evil spirit on Saul, causing him to want to kill David? (1 Samuel 16) All of the Psalms written by David were inspired by David's storms. Out of his storms, David could testify about God's power to deliver His people. In life's storms you learn that God has the power to deliver.

▲ What if God hadn't sent Elijah to ask the widow of Zarephath for her last bite of food? What kind testimony would she have? She never would have experienced a pot that never runs out of meal or a jar that never runs out of oil. (1 Kings 17)

▲ What if God hadn't allowed Peter, or Paul and Silas to go to jail? (see Acts 16) By allowing them to be incarcerated, and then miraculously setting them free, God demonstrated that He would be with them at every turn. These experiences gave them strength to endure the persecutions that were sure to come.

In every one of these circumstances, it was God who put these people in their storms, even though the challenges made no sense to them. Storms never make sense to us. We think we want life simple and easy, without struggle or conflict. But life is never that way, so doesn't it seem reasonable that God would allow us to go through some directed storms?

RELATIONSHIP

Verse 48 of Mark 6 reveals that Jesus was about to pass by them. Think about that. The disciples were in the boat hollering, screaming, and carrying on something fierce, trying to keep the boat from capsizing. They were scared to death but they noticed that Jesus was about to walk past them. Although we know from God's Word that He will never abandon us, the disciples' experience on the boat that day, as well as our own life experiences, help us to understand why Fanny Crosby was inspired to pen the lyrics "Pass Me Not, O Gentle Savior": "While on others thou art calling, do not pass me by."

We need to know who we are as Christians. The brother of the prodigal son got mad because they were having a "welcome home" party for his wayward brother (Luke 15). But the father reminded him that he had the benefit of his blessings all along. If you believe in Jesus, then by adoption you are a child of God, His heir. But if you don't avail yourself of your Father's power, don't get mad at anybody but yourself!

Having God's power available to you is like this. Imagine that you're standing at the bus stop and it's pouring down raining. You're soaking wet with no umbrella. All of a sudden, you see your brother pull up at the red light. But the light changes and your brother is about to pull off. What would you do? Most likely, you would call out or throw something at the car to get his attention before he has a chance to pull off. You might shout, "Hey, Brother! Stop the car! Give me a ride home!" You approach the car with expectancy and a sense of entitlement because that's your brother. There might be other folks at the bus stop who are soaking wet too, but they can't call on your brother like that because they don't know him. They don't have a relationship with your brother.

It's the same way with those who believe in Jesus. If you have accepted Him as your Savior, it gives you entitlement to call on Him when you need Him. Because of your adoption you have a right to say "While on others thou art calling, do not pass me by." Only a child of God can call on Jesus like that. You need to know who you are and what you're entitled to according to His promise.

In order to get through the storms of life, you have to know what it means to be a child of God. You can't make it through the storms of life with your own strength. You need to know with certainty that you can call out to Jesus and say "Hey! Can't you see I need some help over here?"

To Glorify Himself

God is not going to send you into a storm in order to watch you fail. Jesus knew from the outset that the disciples would make it out of the storm. He had already given them the assurance that they would make it to the other side of the lake. In other words, although they were in the midst of a storm, and it seemed like Jesus was passing them by, they were traveling in His providence because He had already promised that He would meet them on the other side. In Mark 6:45, Jesus told His disciples to go ahead of Him and He would meet them in Bethsaida. Therefore, Jesus didn't need to stop and do anything because they already had His assurance that they would get to the other side. All believers should know what it means to walk and live in God's providence, even in the midst of a storm.

Furthermore, we have to remember that in verse 46, after Jesus sent them on a boat, He went on the mountainside to pray. Could it be that He was praying for them? Praying to the Father for them to have strength to make it through the storm? Praying for God to give them the ability to see His delivering power?

Jesus had to know they were about to go through it. Do you think He would send them out there without praying for their safety, for their strength, and their faith? Remember, Jesus knew He was soon going to leave them. He had to strengthen their faith before He could leave them. Even when God sends us in a storm, He does not send us ill equipped.

Therefore, if we accept that Jesus prayed for them, we have to understand that He couldn't just step in and take over when the situation got a little tough. He had to let them struggle before He stepped in. Struggling is simply a part of the Christian journey. In the struggle, we are made strong. From the challenge, we gain personal knowledge of God's sovereignty and power. During the hard times, we learn to trust in the One from whence comes our help, and as we make it through the struggle, we learn just what God can do.

When Jesus stepped in the boat, the storm died and the disciples were amazed. But why? They had just seen Jesus feed more than five thousand people, but they were amazed that a man—they didn't yet know that man was the Messiah—could walk on water and calm the sea. Notice that Jesus didn't calm the water until *after* He climbed into the boat. Jesus can handle the storms. He can handle the storms of your life. Your storms can't topple Him. Your storms can't drown Him. Your storms can't overtake Jesus.

The disciples were amazed because their hearts were hardened. Don't let your heart be hardened to what Christ can do in your life. Let Him have His way with you. Trust Him to see you through the storms of your life. And when He does, give Him the glory. Don't try to pretend you did it all yourself. Give Him the glory and the praise for what He has done. Praise Him that He's strengthening you through the storm, and praise Him when He delivers you out of the storm.

Have you ever gotten mad on the job or at school when someone tried to take credit for your work? Don't you think it bothers God when His people don't give Him credit for what

He has done? It stands to reason that when we trivialize what He has done for us, God is displeased.

While the Twelve were in their storm, they thought they had to get themselves out of that storm. They didn't know that Jesus already had already planned and purposed to see them through. The disciples didn't know where Jesus was, but they were never out of His sight.

You may wonder where Jesus is when you're going through your storm, but be assured that you're never out of His sight. We don't need to know where He is, but we can take comfort in knowing that He is always where He's supposed to be. More important, it's not necessary for believers to know where Jesus is. Even when we can't trace Him, we can trust Him. Trust Him to see you through the storm. Through every situation, through every trial, through every tribulation, through every circumstance, through every storm, through it all—trust Him to see you through.

TRUST GOD THROUGH LIFE'S STORMS
Questions

1. Have you ever experienced a storm in life, even though you were certain you were going in the direction God wanted you to go? How did that realization affect your relationship with God?

2. Why do you believe the Lord deliberately sends His followers into a storm?

3. Do you believe our testimonies are strengthened by the difficult times God sees us through? Explain your response.

4. How can a believer be certain of God's presence while in the midst of a storm?

5. Some believe that as long as they are in the will of God they will not encounter storms in life. Why are they headed for spiritual trouble?

6. Why is our testimony such an important part of the Christian faith, as well our ability to witness to nonbelievers?

7. Is your faith in God rooted in a sense of entitlement as a child of God? How does knowing that you are His child impact your belief regarding what He will do in your life?

8. What advice would you give to a Christian who is angry because he or she has not received certain blessings while less faithful persons seem to receive an overflow blessings?

9. How can you walk in the promise of God's providence, even when you are in the midst of a storm?

10. How has God equipped you for the storms of life? What assurance do you have that He will further equip you for any future storms of life?

11. Draw a line down the center of a sheet of paper. On the left side of the line, write "Storms." On the right side, write "Blessings or Benefits." Under the "Storms" column, write down a few key words that will remind you of a difficult period in your life. In the "Blessings or Benefits" column, list the positive outcomes of that struggle.

12. Say a prayer of thanksgiving to God, praising Him for the benefits and blessings that have come only through struggle.

CHAPTER THREE

Play the Hand Life Deals You

A STUDY OF human behavior reveals a most fascinating phenomenon. For some reason there are people who, though they are born into the most adverse circumstances of life, they flourish and prosper. There are others who, though given every conceivable human advantage, crumble under the challenges of life until they are little more than a pitiful mass of walking flesh.

It has been said that life is like a card game, and human beings must play, to the best of their abilities, the hand that has been dealt to them. Sometimes life deals us a shabby hand, or a hand that it would seem has no value or redeeming purpose, like the accident that left a young and vital Christopher Reeves confined to a wheelchair.

The Book of Exodus reveals that life had dealt the Hebrews a shabby hand, indeed. Exodus 1 reveals the unfolding of their demise. As they grew in number, their worth and stature continued to plummet. Verse 11 says that Pharaoh had put slave masters over the Hebrews to oppress them with forced labor. Yet the more they were oppressed, the more they multiplied and spread; so the Egyptians came to dread the Israelites and worked them ruthlessly. The Egyptians made their lives "bitter with hard labor in brick and mortar" and with all kinds of work in the fields; in all their hard labor the Egyptians used them "ruthlessly" (v. 14, NIV).

Generation after generation of Hebrews knew life to be no more than hard labor and oppression. They were no more than worker ants building cities and monuments to the Egyptian king.

But Chapter 2 of Genesis tells us that a man and a woman from the tribe of Levi married. Surely as they married they hoped to glean a few moments of happiness in their family. They probably hoped that their family would serve as some sort of solace amid the drudgery that they knew a slave's life to be. The life of a slave held little value. They were worked as hard as they could, for as long as they could. The hard labor that the Hebrews endured under the Egyptian pharaohs meant that most of them probably had short life spans. But if a premature death sentence at the hands of the pharaohs were not enough, one pharaoh decided that all of the male Hebrew babies had to die because the Hebrew population was growing at such a rapid pace.

The pharaoh of ancient Egypt was an absolute monarch, the supreme commander of the armies, chief justice of the royal court, and high priest of all religion. The title pharaoh meant "great house." His sovereign power may be understood in that justice in Egypt was defined as "what Pharaoh loves," and wrongdoing was defined as "what Pharaoh hates." The great Pharaoh who ruled over Moses' parents had determined that all male Hebrew babies had to be cast into the Nile River. Egypt's king determined that he would control the slave population in his land by killing off the males. Pharaoh was shrewd enough to recognize he could not afford to allow a nation of strong young men to grow and develop right under his nose. Pharaoh thought he was running the show.

Knowing who runs the show is essential to our strategy for living in the game of life with the hand that life deals us. Pharaoh thought that he was running the show, but a slave woman, the mother of Moses, had another plan. What happened to cause this slave woman—a nobody, a slave, a woman to boot—to defy the great ruler Egypt, a man who by his word could have issued her an immediate and torturous death sentence? How did she dare by her actions say, "You may call the shots in Egypt, but you will not have my child!"? As thousands of Hebrew slave women obediently cast their male babies into the river, one mother had the audacity to defy Pharaoh's edict and hide her baby.

God had planted a seed of defiance in that slave woman's heart that emboldened her to assert: "You may have other babies, but you will not have mine." She hid him as long as she could. When she realized he was getting too big to keep hidden, she got a papyrus basket and coated it with tar and pitch. She then placed the child in the waterproofed basket and placed it among the reeds along the bank of the Nile. The text makes no mention of Moses' father playing a role in the plan. It was his mother who dared to go against the law of Pharaoh. The child for whom she had writhed in pain to bring into the world would not be cast into the water.

The Bible tells us how Moses was drawn out of the river and Pharaoh's daughter found him. But there must have been more going on here than the text reveals specifically. For instance, surely Moses' mother and his sister Miriam knew the time that the Egyptian princess normally took her bath in the river. So on the day they placed Moses in the river, Miriam may have been strategically crouched among the reeds on the bank of the Nile, watching the basket that held her baby brother.

Miriam seized a moment of opportunity, a seizure that impacted two nations of people in a profound, life-altering way. The end of the Israelites' 400-year tenure as slaves was set into motion when Moses' mother and sister conspired to seize their moment of opportunity. It is important that we seize life's important moments of opportunity. These defining moments can have lifelong consequences for good if we allow them:

▲ Like the moment Hannah decided that her husband's other wife, Peninnah, would torment her about her barrenness no longer.

▲ Like the moment that Esther decided to go before the king, even if it cost her life.

▲ Like the moment that Ruth decided to follow Naomi instead of Orpah.

▲ Like the moment Jezebel decided to threaten the life of the prophet Elijah.

▲ Like the moment when the mother of our Lord told the angel Gabriel, "I am the Lord's servant. May it be to me as you have said."

▲ Like the moment Rosa Parks refused to give up her seat on a Montgomery city bus.

▲ Like the moment that Martin Luther King Jr., delivered his "I Have a Dream" speech at the March on Washington.

Thank God that there have always people in life who are willing to move beyond fear and personal consequences and say, "It's time for a change." The reality is that most people are willing to accept the status quo. It's familiar. It's safe. It's predictable. It's normal. They choose comfort and safety over daring and risk. Comfort is a severe deterrent to risk-taking. Often people allow age and a perceived sense of security to pull them away from taking risks. They'd rather be safe than sorry. They believe that a bird in the hand is better than two in the bush.

The women of Moses' family were willing to put personal risk and comfort aside in order to spare the life of young Moses. Their brave actions brought freedom for an entire nation. The actions of these two slave women should remind all believers that none of us should downplay the influence we can have on others. They were just slaves. They were only women, yet their courageous acts yielded a deliverer to free their people from bondage and oppression. Their faithful courage should serve as an inspiration to anyone who doubts a personal sense of empowerment. With God's help, anyone— slave or free, male or female, rich or poor—can be an agent of change for the good of humanity.

Moses' sister placed herself among the princess's attendants and watched as her heart melted at the sight of the crying baby in the basket. Now the princess thought she was running the show as she determined to raise the baby she had "found." The princess named the baby Moses because she had drawn him out of the water. Meanwhile, Miriam had conveniently postured herself to pose the right question at the right time. She asked, "Well, shall I go and get one of the Hebrew women to nurse the baby for you?" And the princess answered, "Yes, go." Miriam went and got her mother. When she arrived, Pharaoh's daughter said to her, "Take this baby and nurse him for me, and I will pay you." Moses' own mother took him and nursed him. So Pharaoh's daughter was paying Moses' own mother to care for him! While other Hebrew mothers were bemoaning the fact that they had drowned their baby boys in the sea, Moses' mother was being paid to care for her own son. Who was really running the show? Moses' mother played the hand that life had dealt her and used it to make a blessing for herself and her family.

So often we tend to look at the negative circumstances of life and allow them to determine our path. When we look at our problems from our own perspective, we think that we don't have the wherewithal to accomplish anything worthwhile. But our little is much in the hands of God.

In the game of poker, the ability to "bluff" is an essential element of the game. In the Christian context, we can think of it as walking in faith. In large measure, faith means believing to such a strong degree that we behave like the victory already has been won—and it has. A famous rapper once told how he got his first recording contract by making the record company executives believe he already had a quality portfolio of songs to produce a CD. In reality, however, he only had one song, which he played for the executives. They believed him and signed him to a recording contract immediately. Once the deal was sealed, the rapper went into the studio and produced a full CD, which became a huge hit.

Similarly, in 1993 the creators of the FUBU® (For Us By Us) line of clothing presented their line to a number of distributors and clothing chains. They convinced retailers that they could meet the production demands if they agreed to carry the FUBU® line, which at that time primarily consisted of caps. The FUBU® creators, Daymon John, J. Alexander Martin, Keith Perrin, and Carl Brown, didn't have a factory to make their wares. Their first "factory" was a basement in their Queens neighborhood. The FUBU® creators took their first ten shirts and had rappers wear them for publicity. Then they took the shirts back, dry-cleaned them and put them on other rappers who were making videos. In 1995, the creators went to a trade show to show the clothes they had made so far. At the show, buyers came into the room, looked at the rack of clothes and placed an order. Soon, they had their first $300,000 in orders. The five young men had taken what they had available to them and made it work.

When we allow God to "call the shots" and run our show, we automatically become more skillful at playing the game of life. Consider the two women, Shiprah and Puah, the Hebrew midwives who refused to kill the male Hebrew babies, even after Pharaoh commanded them to do so. The midwives, however, feared God more than they feared a human being and did not do what the king of Egypt had told them; they let the boys live.

When Pharaoh found out that some Hebrew boy babies were still being born, he summoned the two midwives and asked them, "Why have you done this? Why have you let the boys live?" The midwives answered Pharaoh, "Hebrew women are not like Egyptian women; they are vigorous and give birth before the midwives arrive." Because they feared God, He was kind to the midwives and the Hebrew people increased and became even more numerous. Because the two women feared God, the Lord gave them families of their own. God was running their show, not Pharaoh.

If you think that the circumstances of your life are all up to you, then you're destined to fail. But if you entrust your life to God, you are promised success as God sees fit.

Playing the hand life deals you requires that you observe certain rules. First, you need to maintain a certain posture. In a card game that posture is known as the "poker face." If you have a dream, a goal, or a vision that God has placed in your heart, you have to maintain a posture that affirms your faith until God puts you in the place where you desire to be. A twisted or downcast posture only reveals to others that you don't believe you hold a winning hand in life. When you have God on your side, you always have a winning hand. Always strive to carry yourself in a way that affirms your faith in God.

Second, you must watch how you talk. Positive people speak positive words. Complaining and lamenting have no place in the heart of a person who is determined to win, even if that person is holding what appears to be a shabby hand. When people talk incessantly, they may reveal their hand too soon. Consider the circumstances surrounding the lives of Naomi, Ruth, and Boaz. Poor Boaz thought that he was doing something on his own when he became determined to be Ruth's kinsman-redeemer. But Naomi had it planned from the beginning. She told Ruth what to do, and these two women went from poverty to luxury. Many men have stood at the altar and wondered how they got there! While it didn't appear that these two widowed women held winning hands in life, they turned their circumstances into victory.

Likewise, many people may look at another person and wonder, how did they got that job? How did he find that wife? How did they get that house? Often, if not most of the time, human accomplishments are not so much about ability but whether the persons involved allow God to use whatever we have to His glory. Little is much in the hands of God.

Third, you must remember that God has a sense of humor. The Lord often issues justice, mercy, and grace with humor. God smiles, and His people are allowed to smile as they observe the miraculous handiwork of God in their lives. Little is much in the hands of God. Because you believe in God, your circumstances do not determine your fate.

If you believe in Jesus Christ, your circumstances cannot determine your fate. Jarena Lee, first woman to petition AME church for permission to preach, did not let her gender or the times determine her fate. She preached the Gospel to all who would hear. Little Ruby Bridges, who was just a little girl when she marched into her New Orleans school by federal marshals, determined that the vicious racists who surrounded her would not cause her to sink to their level. It's a shabby hand when a little black girl has to face jeers and taunts of angry, ignorant adults simply because her parents wanted her to have a decent education. All the while she walked past the racists who tried to intimidate her, she was praying for them. As she walked, her lips moved in prayer for the people who despised her.

Are you allowing your circumstances to determine your faith? Or are you living in faith, keeping your face and posture filled with faith and expectancy?

When Joni Erikson Tada was 17 years old she was in an accident that rendered her a paraplegic. For thirty years she's been living paralyzed in a wheelchair. Regarding her painful condition that has drawn her to God, Tada says, "I would rather be in this wheelchair knowing God than on my feet without Him."

On Joni's wedding day, she recalled going down the aisle, looking lovingly in the eyes of the man who was about to become her husband. Partway down the aisle, her wedding dress was caught in one of the wheels of her chair and her beautiful white dress became soiled with black streaks. At that moment, Joni made a choice: she would not focus her attention on the stain; she would look down the aisle at her groom, the man who was willing to accept her unconditionally, and keep rolling down the aisle. Life had dealt Joni a difficult hand from an early age; however, she turned her circumstances into a life that gives glory to the Father.

Life can deal any one of us a difficult hand. We can't control the circumstances that life brings to us; however through faith we bring out the fullness of those circumstances and live a life that gives blessings to us and glory to God.

PLAY THE HAND LIFE DEALS YOU
Questions

1. Have you ever known someone who rose to success despite overwhelming adversities? To what did they attribute their success?

2. Have you ever felt as though life has dealt you a shabby hand? How have you tried to rise above those circumstances to achieve your goals?

3. If you had been Moses' birth mother, do you think you would have had the courage to defy the orders of Pharaoh? Why do you think people of such ordinary circumstances are able to demonstrate great internal strength and determination?

4. Have you ever been in a difficult situation that was out of your control yet remained at peace because you knew who was really in control of things? How does knowing who's in control give you peace?

5. Why is it important for Christians to seize their moments of opportunity?

6. Have you ever looked at the negative circumstances of life and allow them to determine your path? What was the outcome of that situation? Were you able to move beyond those negative circumstances to a more powerful stance?

7. What helps you to maintain a faith posture when you are faced with uncertainty or risk?

8. Do you ever monitor how you talk to yourself? For one day only, keep a log of it. In one column, write down how many times you speak negative, disempowering messages to yourself. In the second column, list how many times you speak words of empowerment and faith to yourself. After the day is over, determine whether the majority of your "self talk" is positive and empowering or negative and self-defeating.

9. Do you believe that your circumstances do not determine your fate in life? Recall a time when you were in negative circumstances, yet you continued to believe in something better.

10. Have you ever had a life-altering experience, like Joni Erikson Tada did? How have you moved beyond that experience to live a whole and productive life?

CHAPTER FOUR
Believe You Can Triumph Over Adversity

— MARK 15:21-37; 16:1-8 —

THEOLOGIAN Dr. James Cone said the Gospel is a not a story of success, but rather one of failure—although it is a story of ultimate success. But the story of Jesus of Nazareth, son of Joseph the carpenter and Mary—without the resurrection—is the story of a smart, promising young Jew who had special gifts. He could handle the Scriptures with the best and brightest theological minds of His day. This young man had great potential to be the One who could lead the Jews to overthrow the Roman government and restore the United Kingdom. He had even been pegged by many to be the promised Messiah—the Savior of Israel. He was a great teacher, charismatic and influential. He had the ability to persuade and lead people. He had demonstrated the ability to avoid the legal traps laid for him by the Jewish legal community.

At the triumphal entry into Jerusalem, many were there lining the road, shouting "Hosanna," meaning "Save now!" Through Jesus of Nazareth, the people were looking for immediate relief from Roman oppression. But instead of a victorious overthrow of the Romans, the promising young man from Nazareth ends up being condemned to die on a cross. In the end, His inner circle of disciples abandoned him and the very crowds who cheered him into the city then condemned him to die a criminal's death on the cross.

However, what seemed to be the failure of a man was actually God's perfect attempt to restore humanity unto Himself. Christ is the appropriate offering for resurrection of the relationship between God and humanity. Throughout human history, God has made many attempts to reconcile humankind to Himself because of His great desire for fellowship with us. God's attempts at resurrection and restoration of His broken fellowship with humanity can be seen first in the story of Cain and Abel. God has made such attempts through human failures since history's first brothers. In Genesis 4, both brothers were asked to bring an acceptable offering to God. That offering was God's attempt to redeem humanity. But the two brothers, since they were human, failed. The murder of Abel represents the failure of humanity's first offer for reconciliation.

God's second attempt at reconciliation can be found in the story of Abraham (Gen. 15:10). This episode represents another human failure wherein God attempts to restore relationship between Himself and humanity through a covenant with Abraham, but Abraham fell asleep. The divine restoration process continued through Abraham's lineage—Isaac, Esau, and Jacob. Abraham's progeny would represent the third failed attempt at reconciliation.

Given these experiences, one could perhaps interpret the life of Jesus of Nazareth as simply another failed attempt on the part of humanity to be restored to God. The account of failure is further seen in the questioning of those who were considered Jesus' most loyal followers. Consider the day of Jesus' baptism. In the Gospel of Luke (3:21-22), John the Baptist baptizes Jesus and sees the Holy Spirit in the form of a dove, affirming the divinity of Jesus. Yet even after John has seen tangible evidence in the form of the Holy Spirit, after he went to prison he still has doubts about the identity of Jesus. He sent a letter from jail asking, "Are you the one who was to come, or should we expect someone else?" (Matthew 11:3, NIV). From the perspective of outsiders, Jesus' ministry was filled with doubts and doubters. John the Baptist might have become a staunch follower of Jesus' earthly ministry despite his doubts, but then He was killed—another failure in Jesus' ministry.

There are times in life when it seems like the bad guys are always winning. When we are working in earnest for the Lord, following the vision He has given us, we are often left to wonder, "Who is on the Lord's side?" Jesus was on a mission. His inspiration to endure all that He would experience was fueled by a calling from His Father. Jesus had an enormous task—to complete the plan that would offer salvation to all of humanity.

God issues some gargantuan-sized callings sometimes, doesn't He? Every person who has ever been given a divinely-inspired vision, calling, or inspiration can attest to feelings of loneliness or abandonment in trying to fulfill the vision. The person possessing the vision wonders if they are different from others:

▲ "Is everybody crazy but me?"
▲ "Am I the one who's nuts and everybody else is sane?"
▲ "Am I the only one who gets this?"
▲ "Why am I surrounded by a bunch of clueless incompetents?"

Jesus' frustrations can clearly be seen in the question He asked of His disciples in the Synoptics (Matthew 17:17; Mark 9:19; Luke 9:41), "How long shall I stay with you? How long shall I put up with you?" (NIV).

Jesus had a number of such experiences with His disciples and others who lacked faith. Consider how they wondered about His power after He calmed the raging storm waters during the storm (Mark 4:39) or when He walked on water and calmed the sea (Mark 6:45-52). Even after they had seen all of His miracles, they still had trouble believing. How could He possibly yield Himself to be the Savior of all humanity when He was surrounded by such doubt and unbelief?

Sometimes it seems as though we are called to perform amid impossible circumstances—that God is demanding that we make bricks without straw. It is at those times that, no matter how certain we are that God has assigned the task to us, we feel like we are failing.

Like our own ministry experiences, Jesus' ministry was filled with highs and lows. Some of His highs were not terribly high, but uplifting nevertheless, like the time He encountered the centurion who had such great faith that Jesus' was amazed (Matthew 8:5-13). Or the time when the one leper out of ten returned to Jesus to thank Him for his healing actions (Luke 17:11-19). And it must have felt great to feed thousands of people from just five loaves and two pieces of fish. Those were all highs along the way of Jesus journey—the people who were converted, like Zaccheus, the woman at the well, Jarius' daughter, and the widow's son.

Every person's ministry or Christian journey has high and low points. Most are not extremely high, nor are they extremely low. But for every person who obeys the call of God there are a few absolute highs and sweeping lows. Jesus was on his way to one of the greatest highs of His ministry. But it soon would be followed by His greatest low.

Arguably, the triumphal entry into the city was a great experience for Jesus. The people were so excited to see Him. How they shouted and praised! From the outside, it seemed that Jesus had arrived. It seemed that He had reached a high plane from which He would never come down. There was just one problem—the reason the people were celebrating Jesus' arrival and His true reason for being there were not the same. The shouters and well-wishers were celebrating what they thought would be Jesus' political takeover of Jerusalem from Roman control, and eventually restore the united kingdom of Israel and Judah. But Jesus was entering Jerusalem to complete His mission, one that would institute an eternal kingdom for all who believe in Him.

How often do people dance, praise and shout when everything at church is going the way they think it should? How many people shout in church for the wrong reasons? How many people praise their pastor for the wrong reasons? Yet as soon as the pastor preaches about something they don't agree with, those same people who were singing, shouting and praising are ready to start a ruckus. How many people are willing to tithe as long as they agree with every ministry project the church sponsors? Yet if a ministry program is initiated that they don't agree with, they cut off their giving as if the money belonged to them, not God?

Every minister knows the highs and lows of doing ministry. Every Christian knows the highs and lows of following Jesus. Discipleship is about highs and lows. Obeying God is often about highs and lows, and Jesus' ministry was no different. The Savior entered the holy city on a high note, but the bottom was about to drop out of Jesus' earthly ministry. But how did Jesus shift from adulation upon His entry into the city to crucifixion in just one week? In one week He went from having adoring fans and believers to facing a hostile crowd of enemies. Except for the triumphal entry, Jesus' last week in Jerusalem was a classic human failure. Looking at His ministry from a purely human perspective, Jesus' ministry was a colossal failure:

▲ He failed to attain the complete allegiance of His disciples, as evidenced by the betrayal of Judas.

▲ He failed to elude capture by the mob that came to the garden of Gethsemane to arrest Him.

▲ He failed to satisfy the high priest's questioning.

▲ Jesus failed to gain acceptance as the Messiah because He did not come back in the way the Sadducees and Pharisees expected. In the Old Testament, the Jewish expectation was that when the Messiah came, He would have to come back as Elijah in a chariot of fire.

▲ He failed to hold His band of disciples together as they dispersed and went into hiding. Peter, who earlier had confessed his belief that Jesus was the Son of God, denied ever knowing Jesus (John 18:15-27).

▲ After He was turned over to the Roman government for prosecution, He failed to convince Roman officials of His innocence.

▲ After He was convicted and sentenced to die, He failed to win the popularity of the people to gain release from His sentence; they chose Barabbas instead (Matthew 27:21-22).

If we didn't know the rest of the story, what a tragic story this would be! After reporting His failure to avoid the death penalty, Mark offers us a glimpse into the crucifixion scene (15:21-24). Along the walk to Golgotha, the place of crucifixion, the Roman soldiers forced a man named Simon, a Cyrenian, to carry Jesus' cross—most likely the horizontal bar of the cross. (This act by Simon, a black man, was often falsely interpreted to justify the slavery of people from Africa.) Simon of Cyrene had to carry the cross because Jesus could not bear it any longer. Jesus could not carry his own cross—another failure! The Romans, most likely, were motivated by their desire to hasten the walk to Golgotha, not by concern for Jesus' condition. Jesus was in a weakened physical condition.

Before a crucifixion took place, Romans often inflicted beatings to make death even more painful and humiliating. Therefore, it is understandable that Jesus was in a physically weakened condition.

In human understanding, Jesus died for His own failure. He died for His failure to overthrow the Roman government. He died for His failure to gain the acceptance of the Jewish hierarchy. And ultimately, He died for His failure to come down from the cross. "He saved others," the crowd observed, "but he can't save himself" (Matthew 27:42, NIV). Jesus had once told Peter that He could call on His Father, who would immediately put more than twelve legions of angels at His disposal (Matthew 26:53), yet He did not call to His Father for help or come down from the cross, despite the jeers and insults of the crowd.

All that Jesus endured during the crucifixion represented human failure. Usually, the crucified person's clothes were given to soldiers to sell. A royal robe had been put on Jesus as a mockery of His kingship. In ancient Rome, the worst mockery a royal ruler could endure was having his robe sold on the open market. The act symbolized that his entire reign and kingdom were failures. Selling off a ruler's garments meant that there was no posterity; there was no dynasty or royal line to carry on because the king's clothing would be sold on the open market to commoners. So the soldiers kept pieces of Jesus' robe to forever remind themselves of his failure to attain the status of a king.

In the midst of all these things happening to Jesus, He emitted a loud cry. Jesus' cry was symbolic of humanity's failure being poured into him. At that very moment, all of the sin and all of the failure from past and future generations was poured into Him. How in the world can a Savior be defeated? Literally, all of the sins of humanity, the failures of previous attempts at restoration and all the hypocrisy of organized religion were heaped upon Jesus at that very moment.

Jesus' cry is further evidence of His messianic failure. Herein was Jesus' own humiliation—and the fair, the only, and the just humiliation for sin is to have a moment in time when even God cannot look upon Himself. God is humanly humiliated by sin. He cannot look at Himself in sin. Therefore, for that moment He has to look away. Jesus is humanly forsaken to capture our redemption . . . for only a moment.

If God could not tolerate sin for even a moment in time, why do we think He can tolerate our sin today? That's why human beings become so uncomfortable when they sin. God cannot look upon us in a sinful state. That is why we cannot stand before God when we sin. That's why we feel bad, can't come to church, and can't stand to talk to fellow church members without feeling guilty—because God can have no part of sin and us. He loves us, but He hates sin.

Even at the point of His death, the account of Jesus of Nazareth could still be considered a story of failure. Therefore, only in the light of the resurrection can Jesus' story be deemed a victory. In our Christian journey our ultimate triumph is not always readily apparent. At times we may feel like utter and complete failures. But by His Word we are assured that there is no failure in those who are faithful and obedient to Him. By His Word we know that no one whose hope is in God will ever be put to shame (Psalm 25:3).

By His Word we also know that Jesus' death was not failure, but rather it was the fulfillment of prophecy. A number of verses found in Psalm 22 (NIV) parallel the events surrounding Jesus' crucifixion, an affirmation of prophecy.

▲ "My God, my God, why have you forsaken me? Why are you so far from saving me, so far from the words of my groaning?" (v. 1).

▲ "All who see me mock me; they hurl insults, shaking their heads" (v. 7).

▲ "He trusts in the LORD; let the LORD rescue him. Let him deliver him, since he delights in him" (v. 8).

▲ "From birth I was cast upon you; from my mother's womb you have been my God" (v.10).

▲ "Do not be far from me, for trouble is near and there is no one to help" (v. 11).

▲ "They divide my garments among them and cast lots for my clothing" (v. 18).

▲ "Posterity will serve him; future generations will be told about the Lord" (v. 30).

▲ "They will proclaim his righteousness to a people yet unborn—for he has done it" (v. 31).

In the midst of all of the seeming failures of Jesus' ministry, amid all of this adversity, comes the ending to the story. The failure of Jesus' ministry ends on Friday—Good Friday. The loud shout is the end of Jesus' life, and the end of His earthly failure as well. But it is the beginning of His eternal triumph.

The triumph in the story begins to emerge as we go to the next scene—the women are on their way to the tomb to anoint Jesus' body. The triumph unfolds out of the women's lack of deterrence by the stone. They knew that the stone would be there. They knew that guards would be there. They even wondered who would roll the stone away. But despite their unanswered questions, the women kept on walking toward the tomb. Without knowing how they were going to get past the stone or the guards, the women just kept on walking. The disciples were hiding out at an undisclosed location, but the women just kept on walking. They had a job to do!

Our faith and our drive to obey God demands that we keep going, despite our unanswered questions. We have to keep going even when obstacles appear. We have to be obedient to God's call, even when we feel as though we have been forsaken.

The triumph of Jesus' ministry continues to unfold at the rolling away of the stone. God had left His Son at the cross to die, but He redeemed His Son by rolling away the stone. God often orchestrates triumph through human activity. The women were coming for one thing, but God sent them for another. They were coming to anoint and honor Jesus' body but God had them there as the first witnesses to the resurrection. That is what happens when we wait it out and keep on coming through adversity. Waiting it out is tough sometimes, even when you know God has called you.

Jesus' mission on earth was an apparent failure, yet He endured to the end and because He endured He now sits at the right hand of the Father at a place of honor. God has a great reward for those who endure until the end.

Because God stepped in to redeem humanity, the stone was rolled away. The women didn't have to do it because God did it. The words of triumph were spoken by God's angel: "He has risen! He is not here" (Mark 16:6, NIV). It had happened just as Jesus had said—in three days He would rise again. The apparent failure of the man from Nazareth had been turned into victory. Triumph had won over adversity! Earlier, Jesus had confessed in faith that He would rise from the dead in three days (Mark 8:31; 9:31; 10:34). But later, in the Garden of Gethsemane He prayed that the cup would be removed. But He stopped short of giving up when He said in Mark 14:36 (NIV), "Not what I will, but what you will." He had spoken in faith when He said, "I'll rise again in three days," but on the cross He cried, "Why have You forsaken Me?" (Mark 15:34, NIV). It is important to remember what you confess in faith because you will need it when you go through adversity.

If you want triumph at game time, you have to have practice speaking in faith. You can't just start speaking in faith when your child goes to jail, or when a loved one gets sick, or when you can't pay your bills. You've got to speak in faith now so that when the time of adversity comes you can draw upon what you have already put into practice—and triumph.

The crucifixion would merely be Jesus' adversity were it not for the resurrection. Yet, conversely, the resurrection would mean nothing to us without Calvary. Jesus' earthly journey means nothing without the resurrection. A great many non-Christian faiths acknowledge Jesus as a great prophet, a wise and gifted man, or even a Son of God. But it is the resurrection that makes Jesus the promised Messiah, the fulfillment of prophecy, the only begotten Son of the Living God. The resurrection is our hope that death is not the end for us. The resurrection is our promise that Jesus is more than one of the prophets or a great prophet. He is our triumph over adversity, not just in death, but in life.

The story of Jesus of Nazareth is more than a series of events to commemorate once a year. Jesus' life and ministry is a story on how to live through adversity and eventually triumph. Life brings us both adversity and triumph, and those of us whose hope is in the Lord will triumph if we endure until the end. Jesus doesn't need a memorial because He lives. And because He lives, we can experience triumph over adversity. We can look beyond negative circumstances, unbelievers, detractors, "haters," and enemies who are determined to get us off track. We have a Savior who has personal experience with turning adversity into triumph because He endured until the end.

PRAISE GOD FOR EVERYTHING!
Questions

1. Do you believe it is possible that many of the people who were shouting "Hosanna!" on Palm Sunday were some of the same people who were shouting "Crucify Him!" on Good Friday? Explain your response.

2. Why does Jesus' death represent human failure?

3. Do you experience times when it seems like the bad guys are always winning? How do you affirm in your faith that God is always in control?

4. Why do you think Jesus' disciples had such a difficult time believing in Him even though they had seen Him perform many, many miracles? Why do you think it is difficult to maintain faith in Him today, even though we know about so many of the great miracles He has performed?

5. What have been some of the high and low points of your walk with the Lord? How has your relationship with Him been sustained even through the ups and downs of life?

6. How did Jesus' life shift from adulation upon His entry into the city to crucifixion?

7. Have you ever been mocked for being a Christian? Have you ever been ridiculed for your faith because God did not act in your life when someone else thought that He should? How have you maintained your faith during such times?

8. When you cry out to God, as Jesus did, what gives you assurance that God hears your cry?

9. Recall a time when God turned adversity into triumph in your life. Thank Him for His faithfulness to his people.

10. What gives you strength to keep going, even when obstacles appear? How are you able to remain obedient to Him, even when you feel forsaken by Him?

11. The women who went to anoint Jesus' body kept going even though they had no idea how they would get the entrance stone rolled away. Have you ever simply kept going, even though you had no idea how the thing you were moving toward would come to fruition? What was the outcome of your situation?

12. Why does the hope of every Christian lie in the resurrection of Jesus Christ? Spend some time praising God for His loving sacrifice for all humanity.

CHAPTER FIVE

If You Have the Gift, You Have to Use It!

— ESTHER 4:5-16 —

THERE IS A story about four people—Everybody, Somebody, Anybody, and Nobody. There was an important job to be done and Everybody was sure that Somebody would do it. Anybody could have done it, but Nobody did it. Somebody got angry about that because it was Everybody's job. Everybody thought that Anybody could do it, but Nobody realized that Everybody wouldn't do it. It ended up that Everybody blamed Somebody when Nobody did what Anybody could have done.

There are times in life when everybody indeed knows that something needs to be done, but it seems that no one wants to step up to the plate and finish the job. That was the case when there was a serious plot to annihilate all of the Jews living under Persian rule. Somebody had to do something do keep this terrible thing from happening.

Some believers think that the Book of Esther should not be in the Bible. The name of God is not mentioned, although the providence of God is interwoven throughout the story. Yet from Esther's experience comes the Feast of Purim, which is still observed by the Jews to this day.

The story of Esther has all the intrigue of *Arabian Nights*. It is a love story and it is a mystery. Most of all, it is a story of triumph for God's people. Through our examination of the story of Esther—whose Hebrew name was Hadassah—we can know that even then our God was faithful to His people, making a way out of no way, putting people in the right places at the right times, pitting the powerless against the powerful. Surely you can recall times when the Lord just worked something out for you? You don't know how He did it, and you didn't know when He was going to fix it. The only thing you know is Who straightened it all out.

Something needed to be straightened out for the Jews. It was time for a change, Things were bad for the Jews. Haman, a nobleman in the court of King Xerxes, was angry at Esther's cousin Mordecai. Because of his faith in God, Mordecai had refused to bow and pay honor to Haman. His rebellion made Haman angry and he grew to dislike Mordecai intensely. He wanted revenge against Mordecai for his open display of rebuke. But Haman's rage was not confined to one man; he grew to hate all Jews and vowed to kill all of Mordecai's people. Something had to be done and Mordecai knew that his niece Esther was just the person to do it. She had the gift, and she needed to use it.

Esther was nobility in exile. She had become the queen, the wife of King Xerxes, yet she belonged to an exiled people. (Our circumstances should never define who we are.) She was able to rise to the level of queen in a land where her status had been just above that of a slave. Her cousin Mordecai had adopted her and trained her in the ways of Judaism. You have to admire Mordecai—a godly, discerning man of conviction. Obviously, he was not so concerned with being in the limelight but was content to work steadily to put things into motion. Mordecai would not compromise himself or his beliefs by bowing to Haman. His concern was not simply for himself; Mordecai was concerned with insuring the safety and security of his people.

Whenever you put the work of the Lord before humankind, the devil gets mad and tries to destroy your work. But God always has a plan. God positioned Esther to become the next queen and thereby save her people. He elevated her for a purpose. Her blessing was to serve a greater good. That is always a barometer for the blessings we desire from the Lord. We should always question whether what we seek from God will serve as a blessing to others as well.

God positioned Esther to save her people, but she didn't simply stumble into the blessing of being queen. Esther did some things that allowed God to position her in the place where she needed to be.

PREPARE YOURSELF

There were several young women to be considered for the position of queen, as King Ahasuerus (Xerxes I) had deposed Queen Vashti for her failure to comply with his request to present herself at a royal feast. The king would have his pick from a stable of young women who would present themselves to him in what amounted to a modern-day beauty pageant. But not just any young woman could join the pageant ranks. Before a young woman's could to be presented to the king, however, she had to complete twelve months of beauty treatments prescribed—six months with oil of myrrh and six months with perfumes and cosmetics. Esther was a beautiful young woman, so beautiful that she was readily chosen to be a candidate for Xerxes' new queen. But Esther didn't rely simply on her natural beauty to position her as the new queen of Persia. Despite her natural physical attributes, Esther was willing to submit to the beauty regiments and listen to the dictates of the eunuch assigned to her.

So many people desire to be elevated to a higher status or circumstance in life, but they may not be willing to do what is necessary to get there. The truth has often been said, "There's no such thing as an overnight success." All of the people we see on television or at the movies or the theatre or even in the pulpit have paid dues or sown seed to get there. Oleta Adams, a popular singer, commented that she laughed when people began calling her an overnight success after her first hit CD. She recalled, "They didn't see all of those times when I was singing at some Holiday Inn lounges in Nebraska!" Rarely do people see the climb, the struggle, or the sacrifice that was an inherent part of another's success. They see the end result and tend to think that it was easy getting there.

People may observe your giftedness, and even desire to emulate it, but rarely are they willing to pay the price. There's a story about an accomplished pianist who was giving a concert in New York. At a reception following his concert, a woman went up to him and said, "I would give anything to be able to play the piano like you do." The man replied, "No you wouldn't." The woman looked puzzled. The pianist explained, "You wouldn't practice for 15 hours a day. You wouldn't practice until your hands become stiff and sore. You wouldn't give up having a social life because you're on the road performing more often than not." The woman admired his gift but in reality she was not willing to make such an investment.

Just because a person is gifted or talented, it doesn't mean that person doesn't have to work at it. Preparation is hard work; it's not glamorous and it's tiresome. Any athlete will attest to the long hours of practice needed before the game is won. Any singer will attest the many hours of rehearsal needed before a performance. Any preacher will agree that the 30-

minute sermon preached in the pulpit is the result of hours, even days or weeks, of preparation.

HEED THE ADVICE OF THOSE IN THE KNOW

When Esther's turn came to go to the king, she asked for nothing other than what Hegai, the king's eunuch who was in charge of the harem, suggested. And Esther won the favor of everyone who saw her. She kept her family background and nationality, just as Mordecai had told her to do. Even though she was about to be queen, she continued to follow Mordecai's instructions as she had done when he was bringing her up.

Nobody is born knowing everything. All of us have to sit at somebody's feet and learn. Joshua sat at the feet of Moses. Samuel sat at the feet of Eli. Elisha sat at the feet of Elijah. Paul sat at the feet of Gamaliel. Everybody needs some training. We all need to listen to somebody in life. The training we need for life is more far-reaching than a formal education. We must listen to the voices of older people in the community. We must listen to the voices of older people in the church. We must listen to the voices of people who have walked on the Christian journey just a bit longer. We need to listen to those in spiritual authority over us.

Esther had natural beauty, but she listened to those who knew more about what she needed to do to get next to King Xerxes. She listened to the advice of her older cousin Mordecai and that of the eunuch assigned to her. She knew that good looks would not be enough to get her into the position of queen. The command was issued in every province to bring all the beautiful girls into the harem at the citadel of Suza. The competition must have been stiff; Esther needed an edge. Her edge was to submit to the wisdom of those who were older, wiser, and more experienced.

Use Your Giftedness to Make a Difference

When we pray for God to bless us through elevation, when He answers the prayer we have to be careful not to believe that that's the end of the story. God doesn't elevate us just so that we can be satisfied with ourselves. He doesn't elevate us just so we can have a more expensive car or a bigger house. Those things are good to have and God wants us to have them; but that's not the reason why He elevates us. God desires that we use our blessings to make a difference in the lives of others.

Esther had moved to the royal palace and was living large. She had people waiting on her hand and foot. Perhaps she thought that she had achieved all that she was to do—but God had a greater purpose for her ascendancy. Perhaps she thought that being queen was enough to bring pride and redemption to her people. And just as she had gotten comfortable with her position, Mordecai threw down the gauntlet. He issued a challenge to her that revealed the true purpose of her blessing.

Naturally, at first Esther didn't want to jeopardize her position with her husband, the king. He had, after all, beheaded his previous wife and she didn't want the same thing to happen to her. But Mordecai wanted to help her take her faith and her consciousness to another level. He wanted her to believe that God could do more than put her in a mansion and give her a title, servants, and jewels. That wasn't the end of her story. Esther needed to use her influence to save an entire nation of people. She was torn. She loved Mordecai. He had devoted his life to her. But at the same time, she didn't want to risk her position in order to get involved. In other words, she didn't want to use the gift that God had blessed her and positioned her to use.

Mordecai was unsympathetic to her predicament. He issued her a challenge: "Do not think that because you are in the king's house you alone of all the Jews will escape. For if you remain silent at this time, relief and deliverance for the Jews will arise from another place, but you and your father's family will perish. And who knows but that you have come to royal position for such a time as this?" (Esther 4:13-14, NIV).

Mordecai's statement was powerful! First, he wanted her to know that being in the king's palace was no guarantee that she would be immune from persecution. We need not think that we're immune from persecution or racism or sexism simply because of what we have achieved. A prominent African-American businessman recalled standing outside a New York hotel wearing a rather expensive navy blue cashmere coat. A white man stepped outside the door and, seeing the black man standing at the curb, asked him to hail a cab. Despite the fact that the black man was a high-powered professional, the white man assumed that the black man in the expensive cashmere coat was no more than the hotel doorman. He thought the blue coat was a uniform!

Shortly after I took a job at a well-known religious publishing company, I went to have lunch in the cafeteria and decided to investigate the salad bar. Although I was dressed in business attire, a white woman wearing jeans walked up to me and told me that they needed more dressing on the salad bar. Her embarrassment revealed that, despite my appearance, she assumed I worked in the cafeteria because I am black. Being in a position of power, influence, or privilege does not exempt you from trouble.

Second, Mordecai wanted Esther to understand that she should not have a false sense of security, thinking that she was exempt from trouble and persecution because she lived in the palace. This is why Jesus warns us not to store up treasures in the things of earth: "Do not store up for yourselves treasures on earth, where moth and rust destroy, and where thieves break in and steal. But store up for yourselves treasures in heaven, where moth and rust do not destroy, and where thieves do not break in and steal. For where your treasure is, there your heart will be also" (Matt. 6:19-21, NIV).

In other words, Mordecai was telling her, "You got the gift, you got to use it!" He wanted her to use her blessings and her giftedness for a cause that was lasting and would bring benefit to someone other than herself. That is, after all, why God gifts us; it is not merely so that we will be satisfied with ourselves. Esther's royal robes, gold jewelry, and crown are long gone. But what remains is her crown of righteousness. The celebration that memorializes her work lives on.

The work of Katy Ferguson lives on. She was the first woman to establish Sunday school classes for black children in America. Born a slave, Catherine "Katy" Ferguson was eight years old when her mother was sold. She never saw her mother again. That permanent separation undoubtedly impressed upon her the needs of desolate children, and they became the great concern of her life. When she was sixteen years old, a woman was kind enough to purchase Katy's freedom for $200. She married at age eighteen and had two children, both of whom died in infancy.

Although she never learned to read, Katy gathered the poor and neglected children of her neighborhood, no matter their skin color, for religious instruction every Sunday at her modest dwelling on Warren Street in New York City. A minister who heard of her work convinced her to move her school to the basement of his new church on Murray Street. Thus, Catherine Ferguson's Sunday school was the first to be established in the city of New York.

But her labor did not end with Sunday school. Twice a week she held prayer meetings for the children and adults in her neighborhood. For over forty years, she continued that work in every neighborhood in which she lived. Over her lifetime took in almost fifty children from living on the streets or from unfit parents. She raised them or kept them until she found suitable homes for them.

The work of many dedicated Christians lives on because they made their treasure the things that last—like Mary McLeod Bethune who devoted her life to Bethune-Cookman College, or James Weldon Johnson, whose lyrics and poetry continue to inspire people of all colors.

Sometimes it's painful to use your giftedness because when you are highly gifted tends to stir feelings of jealousy, envy, or criticism from others. It's difficult to maintain your enthusiasm about what you do when others are looking at you and saying, "Who does he think he is?" or "She thinks she's all that."

Be happy for any person doing any good thing because it may be you trying to do something innovative the next time. Or it could be your daughter or son, sister or brother, or niece or nephew. Do what you're supposed to do and God will work it out.

While Esther was working things out, the Lord moved in. God prepared and paved the way for Esther to approach the king with her request. Esther 6:1 reveals "That night the king could not sleep; so he ordered the book of the chronicles, the record of his reign, to be brought in and read to him" (NIV).

When you step forward, God will move in, clearing the path ahead of you. God cleared the path for Deborah as she prepared to lead an army. He prepared the way for Ruth and Naomi as they returned to Israel in search of a better life. He made a way for Mary, the mother of our Lord, as she consented to risk her life and her reputation in becoming an unwed mother. God made a way for the woman at the well to find salvation and escape from her lifestyle.

Esther 7:10 tells us, "So they hanged Haman on the gallows he had prepared for Mordecai. Then the king's fury subsided" (NIV). God has not changed. Injustice will not stand. But what might have happened if Esther had not been willing to use her giftedness to help her people?

Things are always changing in our world, but the promise of Christ is the same always—yesterday, today, and forever-more. In these modern but uncertain times, we look for assurance, and at times it seems nowhere to be found. We must hold on to God's unchanging hand. No matter what happens to us in life as we know it, we can depend on the Lord to uphold His faithful, to position and empower them, and to bless them to do His work.

If you have not answered your call, what are you waiting for? Are you waiting for things to be safe? Things are never safe. Esther didn't know if she was going to die, and once she became convicted that didn't even matter!

What are you using your giftedness to do? Every Christian is assured by Jesus Christ to receive at least one gift from the Holy Spirit. What is your gift? Do you know that God has put His call on your life? Since He has, you've got to use it. Are you waiting on someone else to do it? Let Him direct your paths and guide you to use your giftedness in this changing world. No matter what happens, God always has work for you to do.

IF YOU HAVE THE GIFT, YOU HAVE TO USE IT!

Questions

1. Think of a time in your life when God simply and divinely worked something out for you. Say a prayer of thanksgiving to God for His power and His willingness to provide all that you need.

2. Why do you believe Mordecai refused to pay homage to Haman? Why is it difficult for most people to take such a strong stand of faith? Name at least one other instance in the Bible when God's people refused to bow down to anyone other than the Lord.

3. What is a reliable barometer for the blessings we desire from God? Are you asking God for a blessing right now? Ask yourself if the blessing would be of benefit to anyone other than you.

4. Have you ever known someone who was jealous of another person's gift or success, even though that person may have worked very hard for their accomplishments? Why do you think some people refuse to acknowledge another person's hard work and preparation, choosing instead to remain full of jealousy and criticism?

5. Why do you think people sometimes believe that if God has already gifted them they don't need to do anything

further to advance or improve their giftedness? How do you think God responds when we continue in measures to advance the gifts He already has given us?

6. How do believers benefit when they listen to the advice and wisdom of older, seasoned Christians? Who have been your resources for Christian wisdom in your walk with the Lord? How have these persons benefited your life?

7. How have older, seasoned Christians helped you grow closer to God?

8. Why are people so seldom willing to sacrifice their personal comfort, even for such a great cause as helping to save scores of human beings?

9. How are you using your giftedness and your blessings to make a difference in life?

10. Why do you think Mordecai was so unsympathetic to Esther when she was reluctant to go before the king?

11. What things have you invested your gifts and your energy into that will live on after you have departed this earth?

12. Recall a time when God stepped in and cleared a path for you, making the way much less difficult than you had imagined. Thank God for His protection and providence.

CHAPTER SIX

Hold on to Your Hope

— JEREMIAH 29:4-14 —

A FAMOUS comedian interviewed on a popular talk show reflected on how black humor was established as its own art form. The comedian shared with the talk show host that Africans were forcibly shipped to the West to be sold in the slave trade. He then shared a story about how, along the Middle Passage, two Africans were lying side-by-side in chains, packed like sardines. Suddenly, one of the two men began to laugh. Curious, the other African asked him, "What's so funny?" The laughing man responded, "Yesterday, I was a king."

Most of us know what it feels like to have our status or life circumstances altered in a negative way. Being thrust into unpleasant circumstances forces us to re-examine everything about ourselves, our lives, and even our God. The sudden shift may be something as simple as having to change our route to work because of road construction. But the experience may be something more traumatic, such as the death of a loved one or loss of income. These life shifts happen to us at every age and in all cycles of life. A toddler begins attending daycare and leaves the sanctity of home. A child moves from elementary classes to the more challenging pace of middle school. A popular high school student graduates only to become an unknown at a large university.

A young person leaves home and has to learn how to budget an income and pay bills responsibly.

Certain life transitions are predictable and expected, yet in every person's life come changes and challenges so traumatic that they could never be anticipated. The more than 6,000 children who lost at least one parent during the terrorist attacks of September 11, 2001 experienced a radical life change that will no doubt affect the rest of their lives. The persons who invested their life savings in the Enron Corporation could never have imagined that one day they would be left in financial ruin. The woman who has been married for 30 years comes home one day to find her husband packing his suitcase because he's moving out.

Great life losses cause human beings to experience feelings of grief, displacement, bewilderment, depression, and loss. The experience can cause many people to re-examine, and in some cases re-identify, themselves. Such experiences can even cause people to question the existence and sovereignty of God and their relationship with Him. In trying and traumatic times, people wonder "Lord, where are You?" or "Why is this happening to me?" or "Father, do You even care?"

Believing that we have been displaced by God or even from God is a form of spiritual exile—feelings of being lost or abandoned without the security of grounding or rootedness. At some point in life, most believers experience spiritual exile when they are removed from a place that is familiar and comfortable—whether that place is physical, emotional, or spiritual—into a foreign place. Our exiles can evoke a range of thoughts, from mildly irritating to downright traumatic and terrifying. As human beings, we tend to define ourselves according to where we are in life and the persons with whom we associate. Therefore, when we are in a mode of questioning who we are or where we stand with God, our very sense of identity is threatened or compromised.

People are often most vulnerable to the temptations of the enemy when their spiritual identity has been compromised. When that compromise occurs because of spiritual exile, people are likely to engage in behavior that is not a part of their normal activities. A gainfully employed, financially stable person might start shoplifting when she is thrust in a period of spiritual exile. A happily married man may resort to an extramarital affair in seeking to avoid the pain of exile due to unemployment.

Israel knew the feeling very well. In 587 B.C., the people were uprooted from the place where they had been born, the place that had belonged to their ancestors for generations, the place that God had set aside just for them, the Promised Land . . . the land that God had shown Abraham hundreds of years before. Israel wasn't just a country to them; it defined the very identity of its inhabitants.

Israel was the place of God's promise—the Promised Land. The land that Abraham's progeny inhabited was both visible and tangible evidence of the fulfillment of God's promise. Furthermore, it stood as a proving ground or a guarantee that God would continue to honor His word to His people. But something happened that no one could have imagined. God allowed His people to be cast out of the land He had given them. Abraham, Isaac, and Jacob had no way of knowing that one day the disobedience of their descendants would reach such depths. When upon his deathbed, Joseph asked that his bones be taken from Egypt and buried in the land God had promised to his forbears, never did he dream that a day would come when they would no longer occupy the land because of their unfaithfulness to God.

Life is full of exilic experiences. We barely get comfortable in one situation before we are forced to deal with a new set of circumstances—new job responsibilities, unemployment, a new supervisor who is less understanding than the old one, a stepchild who moves in and makes life a living hell on earth, new in-laws, a new pastor, a new principal, new neighbors, new construction around the neighborhood, or highway construction that ties up traffic for months, even years. All of these things cause us greater or lesser degrees of discomfort and throws everything out of joint

When we experience personal and spiritual exiles, there are always some lessons we need to remember in order to reap benefits from that experience. The lessons gleaned help lay the foundation for growth and empowerment in our lives.

GOD'S PEOPLE LIVE BY A DIFFERENT STANDARD

The reason for Israel's exile is perfectly clear: Jeremiah, along with and many other of God's prophets, had preached that the nation's stability and security depended on their faithfulness to the God who had brought them to that very land.

God's messages of warning were continually scorned and rejected. After repeated episodes of warning and forgiveness, God could take no more. He allowed Israel to continue along their path of destruction without interruption. One day, the Babylonian army came and captured Jerusalem. After overtaking the city, the Babylonians selected the leading people of the city for deportation. They took Israel's best and brightest. If you want to stop a dog, you cut off the head, not the tail. When you're trying to cripple someone, you take out the thinkers and the strategizers. It has been speculated that the reason why Africa has been relegated as a third world continent is because for 400 years, the nations' best, strongest, and brightest were stripped from countries from east to west. The

Babylonians took out the movers and shakers, those in the best physical shape, the most intelligent, and the most keen to make sure that those left behind would not have the wherewithal to revolt and start anew. Perhaps the Babylonian invaders share a philosophical kinship with W.E.B. DuBois, who espoused the Talented Tenth theory in the early 1900s. DuBois believed that the cream of the crop among Negroes in America amounted to about ten percent of the black population. In a paper written in 1903, titled "The Talented Tenth," he reasoned that this exceptional group of black people would save the race by leading and elevating the black masses away from "the contamination and death of the Worst, in their own and other races." By taking out the best and brightest of Israel, the Babylonians insured that the nation would remain captive in both body and mind.

Although it was the Babylonians who came in and leveled Jerusalem, when the exile came, the Israelites cried out to God, "Unfair!" Immediately, Israel wanted to compare themselves with others. Surely there were others who were doing things worse than what Israel had done. But as they were crying out that the exile was not fair, they failed to acknowledge the fact that God's people live by a different standard. "We weren't perfect, but other people have done worse than the things we did!" they cried.

Have you ever known someone who seems to get away with any kind of deceit, or wrongful deed, and never seems to suffer any direct consequences? Psalms 82 and 94 both ask God why the wicked have not suffered the consequences of their deeds. The prophet Jeremiah asked, "Why does the way of the wicked prosper?" (Jer. 12:1, NIV). It is a question that all godly human beings ask. When we watch people engaging in wicked or evil behavior, we console ourselves by thinking, "Okay, they'll get theirs one day." But some of them continue in their behavior for years with no repercussions. And, as far as we can tell, some never seem to suffer the consequences of their actions. Despite this, during those times that you have chosen to engage in sinful behavior, God may have called you into account more readily.

Perhaps you have watched other people's wickedness and as you observe them you know in your heart that you would never get away with such actions. God's people live by a different standard. God told Jeremiah (29:11, NIV), "For I know the plans I have for you...plans to prosper you and not to harm you, plans to give you hope and a future." God has plans for His people. His plans are not to let you do any and every thing you choose. God has to harness His people for their own protection so they may fulfill His purposes. God has plans for His people to live fully and abundantly (John 10:10).

As Israel moved into Babylonian territory, they were full of complaints like, "It's too hot here," "The food is bad," and "The schools are substandard." Ironically, they now longed for the land that they had, but they had been unwilling to do the things necessary to continue inhabiting the land. While they had inhabited the land, they had steadfastly refused to honor the God who had brought them there. They were wishing for Jerusalem but living in Babylon. They refused to deal with the reality of their circumstances or the very actions that caused them to be in that situation in the first place. The problem was they forgot that God's people live by a different standard. They didn't appreciate Jerusalem enough to honor and worship God when they had it. The Israelites' experience is reminiscent of a couple that got divorced. During the marriage, the husband showed little love, kindness or respect to his wife. Yet a few months after the divorce was final, he wanted his ex-wife to consider reconciliation. The wife refused to reconcile, however; not because she was opposed to the idea of reconciliation but because her ex-husband showed no evidence that he had repented or was willing to honor the marriage covenant. He wanted to regain the benefits of marriage without making any sacrifices. Israel wanted the benefits of living as God's people but was unwilling to be obedient to Him.

FALSE PROPHECIES ARE DANGEROUS

Interestingly enough, as they were escorting away the best and the brightest of Jerusalem, the Babylonians left the prophet Jeremiah behind, though no one knows exactly why. Perhaps his own people had ignored him so long that the Babylonians didn't consider him to be much of a leader, either. Yet the Babylonians did take other religious leaders, including Ahab, Zedekiah, and Shemiah. These prophets were men who called attention to the unfairness of the people's plight and stirred the pots of discontent among them. These three prophets encouraged the people to hang on a little longer because their period of exile wouldn't last much longer. These three prophets claimed to have had God-given dreams that revealed their period of exile would end soon.

Of course this was exactly what the people wanted to hear. We always want to hear that life is easy. We rejoice at good news. We rejoice at the passing of bad times. No one wants to be the bearer of bad news. But God's messengers can never get caught up in telling people what they want to hear—unless, of course, the message is from God. The worst mistake a preacher can make is preaching what folks want to hear and not what God reveals and inspires. Many of God's messengers, fearing job security, have compromised God's Word just to keep a pastorate or position.

The prophets were making a good living by passing out false hopes and dreams. Their messages were false and downright destructive because they interfered with the people's ability to make an honest living. More importantly, these false hopes and dreams were a serious impediment to their spiritual growth and development. As long as the people thought they might be going home at any time, they refused to make any positive contribution in Babylon. It has been observed that, in most penal institutions, the inmates who are most committed to reform or to making positive contributions are those with life sentences and the long-term inmates. Long-term prisoners are motivated to make prison life better because they know they will be there for a while. Inmates who are doing short stints usually don't care much about making changes for the better or having input regarding prison operations.

Since the false prophets had seduced Israel into believing that they wouldn't be in Babylon for very long, naturally they had these kinds of thoughts:

▲ "Why bother to plant gardens? We'll be gone before harvest anyway. We'll surely be gone before the harsh winter comes. It'll be better if we just pick up a few things at the market each day."

▲ "Why should we bother to establish businesses and learn the culture? We'll just do odd jobs here and there to earn a living—just enough to get by on. There's no need for us to put our intelligence and ability in making a Babylon better place. We'd much rather spend our time thinking about how much we can't stand these people!"

▲ "No need to get married and start families, we don't want to raise our children in this godless land. We'll just have casual sexual encounters until we get back to Jerusalem. Then we'll have acceptable courtships with respectable Jews, marry and settle down, and build real families in our own land."

Their false dreams had lulled them into laziness, unproductivity, and downright sinful behavior. By trying to take short-cuts they compromised themselves and showed no faith in

God. The Israelites were behaving like a teenager who's mad because her parents uprooted her just before her senior year in high school and moved the family to another city. She's away from the familiarity of her childhood friends and her old school. Since she only has a year to go in school, she refuses to try out for the cheerleading squad at her new school even though she was a cheerleader before. She refuses to date any of the boys at her school. She dismisses the idea of participating in any extracurricular activities because, after all, she only has a year to go. Because of her refusal to engage herself in her new surroundings, she misses out on some of the greatest events related to her teenage years.

In life there are some people who never try to make the best of their circumstances. These people find something wrong with everything! Nothing is good enough. They refuse to get along with coworkers or participate in social activities related to work. They balk at any new policy or proposal. They refuse to take part in anything that might improve employee morale or working conditions. They complain constantly about the salary or benefits of the job. They use works like "your" or "ya'll" instead of "us," "we," or "our" when talking about projects at work. These same people are always talking about looking for a new job. Rarely do such people find another place to work, however; the problem is not really the job, it's their attitude about the job.

Like the grumbling employee, Israel had decided that Babylon was not good enough and never would be. They didn't want to try and make life better there. They just wanted to put in their time and get out. Many times when we're in less-than-desirable situations, we just want to put in our time and get out as quickly as possible. The false hopes implanted in them by the false prophets had made them lazy. The false prophets had nurtured their self-pity and gave them permission to be unproductive. Their false dreams were leading them to live hand-to-mouth, to be parasites on society—irresponsible in their relationships and indifferent to the reality of their lives.

BLOOM WHERE YOU'RE PLANTED

Just after the Israelites lulled themselves into false fantasies, along came a letter from Jeremiah. He sent his message by two men who had to go to Babylon on official business. On the way, they visited the exiled community. Of course, the people were excited to see the two men and wanted the "low down" on all the news and events back in Jerusalem. But before they could get all the gossip, the men presented them with a letter—it was a message from the true prophet of God. The news from Jeremiah was not light-hearted nor was it encouraging to their current mindset. Basically, Jeremiah told the exiles five important things:

1. *Build houses.* In contemporary language, Jeremiah was telling them, "You are not camping out. Babylon is your home now. It may not be the place where you want to be, but it's home until God sees fit to let you come back to Jerusalem. Get real and make the best of it. Your life is just as valuable now in Babylon as it was in Jerusalem. You didn't choose life in Babylon, but deal with it anyway."

2. *Plant gardens and eat their produce.* "You need to get off your pity pots and excuses and become a productive part of the Babylonian economy. You are not parasites. You are still God's people. Don't expect the Babylonians to feed you and support you. You need to be responsible for yourselves so that you can set a good example for future generations."

3. *Marry and have children.* "The Babylonians are not beneath you. You can't just walk around snubbing them because you don't want to be here. You cannot live

immorally and expect God to bring deliverance to you. Develop real relationships and stop sleeping around with the Babylonians. If they're good enough to lie down with, they're good enough to marry."

4. *Seek the welfare of the city.* "Take time to get to know the city of Babylon. You'll probably find that it's not a bad place to live. In any case, it's where you live now so look for ways to make a positive contribution to the city. Pray for the city's well being. You live in Babylon. Do everything you can to make it the best place possible. This is now your home, too." In the Hebrew text, Jeremiah advises them to "seek shalom," which means wholeness and peace. They were to make every genuine effort to seek the best for the city.

5. *Do not listen to the lies of false prophets.* "Stop listening to snake oil salesmen and con artists teaching quick fixes and pipe dreams. Listen to the truth. You are going to be here for a while!"

When we experience our personal and spiritual exiles, it is our choice how we will deal with them. Our exiles can be terrible or they can be opportunities to make us stronger. A failed marriage can be an opportunity to move to a new city or make new friends who are more rooted in Christ. A job transfer can be a new opportunity to learn new job skills. A new supervisor can be a new challenge to build discipline and faith. An illness can be the catalyst to developing a stronger prayer and meditation life.

God loved us enough to give us the power to choose. We can choose how we react to every circumstance of life. We can choose how to react to disappointment. We can choose how we wish to react to broken dreams. We can choose how we will react to negative circumstances. We can choose how we will react to the blessings in our lives.

No matter what circumstances come into our lives, what we always must choose is to maintain our hope in the Lord, according to the very promise that He gave Israel in Jeremiah 29:11 (NIV): "For I know the plans I have for you . . . plans to prosper you and not to harm you, plans to give you hope and a future." If God allows us to be in an exilic experience, as believers we have to trust that He knows why we are there and that somehow—if we have the right attitude about it—we will benefit from the experience.

Most of us cannot honestly say that we experienced any significant spiritual growth through easy life experiences during which everything just fell into place? Instead, we learn to trust God because when it looked like we weren't going to make it He stepped in and straightened everything out. But we had to go through the experience in order to find that out. We praise God on Sunday or perhaps at any time we just think about it because when it looked like things were about to cave in on us, God came along and placed a firm foundation under our feet and was a fence all around us. But we had to go through it in order to know that. We learn how much God loves us at the time we don't think anybody in this world cares about us. It is then that He sends someone who shows us loving kindness and compassion. But we had to go through it.

God says in Jeremiah 29:13, "You will seek me and find me when you seek me with all your heart" (NIV). In other words, it is when we go through these trying experiences that we begin to look for God. That's when we will seek Him with all of our heart.

The plain truth is, we don't seek God when life is easy and going well! Some of us barely even pray when things are going right. Some of us forget to tithe when our finances are stable. We fail to look at the money as a tithe that belongs to God; rather, we look at it as "extra" money to buy a new outfit or

something for the home. But when we are trying to come out
of a bad situation, that's when we go looking for God!

God says that it's when we're in exile—separated from the
comfort and security of the familiar—that's when we're going
to look for Him with everything we have! As we're trying to
come out, we will find Him. And when we find Him, He's
going to bring us back from captivity—out of those troubling
circumstances. Why? Because God says, "My plans are to
prosper you" (Jer. 29:11, NIV). That's why we have to live
through all things in hope. He allows us to go through some
things because He plans to prosper us. That's why:

▲ You have to work under that nasty new supervisor, and
  be the best, kindest, most loyal employee in the group!

▲ You have to look at that stepchild who's making your life
  a living hell with the love of God!

▲ You have to take the best care of the house you're renting
  even though you want a home of your own!

▲ You have to keep your car, your clothes, and everything
  you own as your best!

▲ You have to treat others with love and kindness, even
  though they seem to be the most irritating, obnoxious
  creatures God ever made!

▲ That's why you've got to respect that mean teacher who
  doesn't give easy grades and insists that you live up to
  your potential!

It's not enough to simply wish for Jerusalem while you're in
Babylon. You have to deal with where you are, faithfully and
with integrity, as you're seeking God to bring you out. Don't
let a bad attitude cut you off from what God wants to give
you. Without the right attitude, regardless of your circumstances, you can't learn from the experience and be blessed.
You can't get stronger, you can't get better, and you cannot

receive God's blessing for you if you refuse to first bloom where you're planted. The dirt may be hard, rocky, and unfertilized, but because you're a child of God you can still bloom where you're planted. Aaron's staff, though it was no more than a dead tree limb, by the power of God budded, blossomed, and produced almonds (Numbers 17:8). God can do anything but fail! Don't spend your life wasting time wishing for Jerusalem while you're living in Babylon. Bloom where you're planted. It's perfectly acceptable to hope and pray for things in your life to get better. The mistake, however, lies in refusing to honor God by living each day to the fullest while we wait in hope for conditions to change.

You can live victoriously, even while you're in an exilic experience. When you're in an exilic predicament, say to yourself, "My present circumstances do not determine my future." Let your enemies wonder why you can hold your head high even when things aren't going the way you'd like. What they can never understand is that the reason you can hold your head up, the reason you can smile when things are not going the way you'd hope, is because your hope is not in your circumstances, but rather in the God whose plan is to prosper you!

HOLD ON TO YOUR HOPE
Questions

1. The Babylonians took Israel's best and brightest. W.E.B. DuBois theorized about a Talented Tenth. How are you using your God-given gifts? Are you using them in ways that are proportionate to the degree to which God has blessed you?

2. Recall an experience in your life when you were made aware that God calls His people to live by a different standard? How did that realization affect your spiritual growth?

3. Have you ever known someone who seems to get away with any kind of deceit, or wrongful deed, and never seems to suffer any direct consequences? Read Jeremiah 12:1-3. Have any of your life experiences caused you to relate to Jeremiah's sentiments in this passage?

4. In what ways has God demonstrated to you His plans to prosper you (Jeremiah 29:11) and give you abundant life (John 10:10)?

5. Have you ever complained to God about your circumstances, even though you knew it was your own actions that had caused those circumstances to come into being? How did God equip you to endure those circumstances?

6. Have you ever stubbornly refused to turn a "lemon" of a situation into "lemonade"? How were you eventually able to turn the situation around?

7. Have you ever known people who refuse make the best out of their circumstances? How do you think their attitudes affects their overall quality of life? How does their attitudes and outlooks affect the people around them?

8. Recall a situation when you were able to bloom where you were planted. How did the situation occur? How were you able to recognize God's hand in your life, guiding you along the way as you worked to make the best of your circumstances?

9. Make two columns on a sheet of paper. On the left, try to list five ways you have grown spiritually through positives experiences in your life. On the right, list five ways you have grown spiritually through negative experiences in your life. Which set of circumstances had the greatest impact on your overall spiritual growth and development? Explain your reasoning.

10. Recall a circumstance in your life that moved you to look for God? In what way did your "looking" for Him change your life and your behavior?

11. Write down the names of three Bible persons whose present circumstances did not dictate the outcome of their future? How can their experiences serve as a testimony of inspiration to you?

CHAPTER SEVEN

Know the Sure Road to Victory

— 2 CHRONICLES 20:1-5, 13-22 —

ONE SATURDAY afternoon I was watching a special segment CNN about the impact of 9-11 (September 11, 2001) on the city of New York, especially the homeless. Prominently featured were an African-American woman and her four children. They were living day-to-day in a shelter. The woman had lost her job and was not receiving child support. She spent her days pursuing leads for jobs and housing. But a regular part of her family's evening routine was going to church. The woman and her children were homeless, yet she regularly went to church with her children to praise the Lord. The living testimony of this woman struck me powerfully. It pulled me out of my own pity pot because this woman and her children were homeless, yet she was praising God. She wasn't worried about how she was going to pay the rent; there was no rent to pay because there was nowhere to stay. She wasn't worried about getting a big screen or Plasma television; there was no electrical outlet to plug it into. Yet she was earnestly praising God. She wasn't trying to decide whether tonight would be taco night or spaghetti. There was no place for her to prepare a meal for her children anyway. As I watched this woman standing in a New York church, singing praises to God, I remember thinking, "Now that's real faith—the kind that moves God."

We all have times when we need to call up the kind of faith that moves God. It's the kind of faith that Hebrews 11:1 (NIV) describes, "being sure of what we hope for and certain of what we do not see." King Jehoshaphat came upon just such a situation while he was ruler of Judah. Essentially, the armies of three nations had combined their military might to attack Judah. When Jehoshaphat got the news, he was scared—and with good reason. Perhaps you know what its like to get the kind of news that scares the living daylights out of you. Fear and panic strike your heart. You may even become immobilized with fear. Your mind starts clicking a series of scenarios as possible solutions. Yet all the while your mind is racing, you know none of them will work.

Still, you know that you're facing a battle. The opposition is so fierce that you know you couldn't win the battle even if Colin Powell himself brought you an arsenal of nuclear weaponry. You couldn't go to the pawnshop and buy a gun, because that won't do any good. It's not that kind of battle. You couldn't win even if Condoleeza Rice personally mapped out a strategy for dealing with your enemy. And the reason you know that none of these weapons and strategies will work is because the battle is fought in the spiritual realm, not the temporal. A major reason why so many people are living defeated lives is because they are fighting their battles in the natural and not the spiritual. They are attempting to use natural weapons to fight a spiritual enemy. Ephesians 6:12-13 (NIV) warns:

> For our struggle is not against flesh and blood, but against the rulers, against the authorities, against the powers of this dark world and against the spiritual forces of evil in the heavenly realms. Therefore put on the full armor of God, so that when the day of evil comes, you may be able to stand your ground, and after you have done everything, to stand. Therefore,

since you can't fight spiritual battles with
earthly weaponry, you've got to employ a different strategy. You fight spiritual battles with
spiritual weaponry.

The king of Judah rightly understood that he could not
fight his enemies using military might—that's why he was so
afraid. Knowing he could not defeat the combined armies of
the Moabites, the Ammonites, and the Meunites with earthly
weaponry, he employed a different strategy. As the story of
Jehoshaphat's experience unfolds, it reveals the steps that the
king took as he traveled the road to victory for his nation.

PRAYER

The people of Judah had faced battle many times. Each and
every time they went into battle, the key to their victory had
been that the power of God was on their side.

After Jehoshaphat collected himself from the shocking
news, the first thing he did was pray. In times of adversity, the
best place to be is on your knees! Before checking their arma-
ment or devising a strategy for defense, the entire land of
Judah submitted themselves to a period of prayer and fasting.
They wanted to get God's attention. But prayer and fasting are
much more than tools for buying divine influence. They are
acts of obedience. It is through prayer and fasting that we align
our human will with the will of God. These disciplines represent the submitting of flesh to the Spirit, just as Jesus did in
Gethsemane.

When faced with impossible odds, King Jehoshaphat
turned his face toward God. Jehoshaphat knew that he didn't
need more weapons. He didn't need more soldiers. He didn't
need smarter generals. Chapter 17 tells us that he already had
a million soldiers. He didn't need more time to devise a plan
of defense. He and his people needed to fast and pray. When

the enemy got ready to attack Judah, Jehoshaphat did not seek his army, he sought the presence of the Lord.

Jehoshaphat's prayer was a masterful appeal that helped to define the circumstances facing God's people. Basically, his petition was based on several key points (2 Chronicles 20:7-12):

▲ God had given that land forever to the descendants of Abraham.

▲ God was indeed able to help them overcome in this situation.

▲ Jehoshaphat and the people had humbled themselves and come into God's own house to seek His help.

▲ It was God Himself who had forbidden the extermination of the very people who were now threatening to destroy Judah.

▲ Now their enemies were attempting to do to the Israelites what the Israelites had been forbidden to do to them.

▲ Judah's enemies should be judged by God.

▲ God was their only hope, and so they had come to Him for help.

PROMISE

After Jehoshaphat and his people prayed and fasted, they were open to hearing an answer from the prophet of God. They had offered their prayers in the temple—God's sanctuary. They had prayed in the very place where God had promised to hear and answer their prayers.

Through God's messenger, Jahaziel, they were given the promise of victory. His message, which came to them under the anointing of the Spirit of the Lord, contained powerful words: "The battle is not yours, but God's" (2 Chron. 20:15,

NIV). God had to show Judah's enemies that they were picking on His people, so it really was God's battle and not Judah's. The Moabites, the Ammonites, and the Meunites were arrogant enough to try and fight Judah although the Lord had spared them for generations before. As the old saying goes, they didn't believe that fat meat is greasy. So God had to show them something!

Throughout the Bible, a word from the Lord is a certainty. God, through His Word has proven that He is faithful to do what He has promised:

> Your kingdom is an everlasting kingdom, and your dominion endures through all generations. The LORD is faithful to all his promises and loving toward all he has made. (Psalm 145:13, NIV)

> "Let us hold unswervingly to the hope we profess, for he who promised is faithful." (Hebrews 10:23, NIV)

A word from God's prophet is certain to come true; however, a word from God's prophet does not always assure victory. In 2 Chronicles 18, Ahab, king of Israel, and Jehoshaphat had formed an alliance against their common enemy. But before going into battle, Jehoshaphat sought confirmation from a godly prophet—in this case was Micaiah, whom Ahab hated because Ahab was wicked and Micaiah was a true messenger of God.

The key to witnessing the handiwork of God lies not in coercion but in affirming and agreeing with His Word and His will. When we learn to apply the promises of Scripture with the proper motivations and attitudes, we will see results. God is not Santa Claus. He is not looking to see if we've been "naughty or nice." He is the loving Father who desires to (Matthew 7:11), " . . . give good things to them that ask him" (KJV). His blessings do not come because we deserve them nor because we have earned them. They come from His loving benevolence.

Although the battle was the Lord's, Jehoshaphat and his people still had to take their positions and be ready to fight. They couldn't just sit around the house and wait for something to happen. But why did they need to go to the battlefield to meet the enemy when they already knew the battle had been won? Jehoshaphat and the people of Judah had to go there and stand to exercise their faith.

In the face of overwhelming opposition, it is more difficult to stand still in faith than it is to take up arms and fight. It is more difficult to stand still in faith than it is to go curse out our enemies. It is more difficult to stand still in faith than it is to go and take revenge. It is more difficult to stand still in faith than it is to devise our own plan of attack. If faith and trusting in God were easy everybody would be doing it.

But we who stand on the promises of God have a firm foundation, indeed. So after we pray and before we praise, we need to be confident that our desires are within God's will and His Word. We can't just pray and ask God for anything we want and then get up and praise Him, thinking it's something He's supposed to do because we prayed for it! God doesn't work like that! When we pray, we should try to discern whether our petition within His will. We should first determine whether our desires are in keeping with His promises. When we receive divine affirmation of His promise, we can go forward praising Him confidently.

PRAISE

Demonstrating praise and thanksgiving to God before the miracle even occurs is perhaps a believer's most powerful expression of faith and trust in God.

1. Hannah knew it, and that's why she could go to the Temple and praise God after she prayed for a son, but before she conceived.

2. David knew it, and that's why he praised the Lord that his son Solomon would build the Lord's temple after he had prayed to build it himself and even though he would not live to see it happen.

3. Job knew it, and that's why he praised the Lord after he had lost practically everything he had but before it was restored to him.

4. Jesus knew it, and that's why He gave praise and thanks to God after He prayed for the food but before the food to feed the 5,000 had appeared.

5. Paul knew it, and that's why he could praise God while he sat in a prison cell—after he prayed but before he knew the outcome of his trial.

A friend was having trouble finding stable employment, even though he has excellent credentials and experience. A CPA with a master's degree in accounting, he already had gone a year without a job. He began referring to his resume as Halle Berry, because every perspective employer talked about how good it looked when they saw it, but he still didn't have a job. As we talked, I shared with him that I didn't think his real problem was not the job market, nor was his joblessness due to the aftermath of 9-11. His battle was of a spiritual nature and could only be fought and won on a spiritual realm. So I asked him, "Can you praise God for the job He's going to give you, even before you get it? Can you get up and shout and praise Him even while you're still in a state of unemployment?" I reminded him that as a Christian he already had God's promise to take care of him, to never leave him or forsake him. Within two weeks he had got not one job offer, but two! He kept on looking for a job and interviewing, but he quit trying to fight a spiritual battle with earthly weapons.

God had answered Jehoshaphat with a promise of victory. But it is Judah's response and Jehoshaphat's subsequent action that are worthy of further attention. Upon hearing God's promise of victory, they began to praise the Lord! The people of Moab were still waiting in the trenches. Ammon was preparing for the battle. The people of Mt. Seir were sharpening their swords. The battle plans were drawn. Alliances had been made. The enemy was just as real and just as ready to fight as they were before God's people began praying. The only difference was Judah now had a promise. They were standing on the promises of God. And the proper response to God's promise is an affirmation of praise to Him!

Jehoshaphat understood what so many people fail to see: when we have the assurance of His promise, we can praise Him for the victory! Upon receiving divine assurance, Jehoshaphat appointed singers to "praise the beauty of holiness" (2 Chron. 20:21, KJV).

Judah's king placed the praisers ahead of the warriors. This is the proper order for spiritual battle. Before you do battle, before you face the trial, before you engage the enemy, you must affirm God's promises with praise. When you're doing battle, you must have the right weapons, but put your praise—which demonstrates your faith—in front of your weapon.

Sometimes God wants you to show Him that you love Him no matter what. He wants you to show Him praise before He even does a thing because that's your sign that you trust Him. It's hard to have a true, intimate relationship with someone who doesn't trust you. You have to prove everything you say to the person before he or she will believe you. God wants true intimacy with you so He wants you to trust Him.

It must be understood that praise was not the prerequisite to Judah's victory; rather it was a response. Nowhere did God tell Jehoshaphat to put the singers first. They were praising God because the victory had already been promised and won. They were praising God because they knew that the battle was the Lord's, not theirs.

Have you ever been relieved to discover that a battle you thought you were going to have to fight belonged to someone else? Maybe it was a battle you discovered your boss was going to have to fight instead of you. Maybe it was a battle with a neighbor, but you found out the codes department would take that battle instead. Maybe it's been somebody disturbing the peace in your family, but somehow God caused them to just go away, eliminating the need for battle. Maybe when you were younger a bully threatened to beat you up, but somebody else stepped in and defended you against the bully.

Jehoshaphat and Judah were not trying to coerce God with songs of praise. They were thanking Him by faith for a victory that not yet been realized. Their praise was an affirmation that they believed God would do what He promised.

Do you know with certainty that God will do what He has said? Can you let it go so God can fight the battle instead of you? Are you weary, worn, and sad because you have been trying to fight too many battles that never belonged to you in the first place? Just think about the lyrics in "I Heard the Voice of Jesus Say":

"I came to Jesus as I was, weary, worn and sad.

"I found in Him a resting place, and He has made me glad."

He can make you glad, like Jehoshaphat and Judah when they realized they weren't going to be defeated. In Christ, there is no defeat. We who live in Christ can live in the knowledge that He fights all of our battles. He fought the battle against our eternal damnation—and won. He fought the battle against death and the grave—and won.

God will fight your battles. When you know that He'll fight your battles you are glad to give Him the praise that He deserves. When He does, it can be somewhat amusing to stand and watch the Lord deal with your enemies in His way. For instance, you may have experienced trying to cause you grief and make you miserable but you faithfully stood back and let God deal with the situation in His way. People will try to destroy your peace and steal your joy. When they do, pray, look for the promise of God in your desires, and give Him praise for the victory. Then watch your enemies fall all around you. They may never even know why they fell. They didn't see you do anything. They didn't see you fighting, clawing, or conniving. All they knew is that they fell and you were still standing. But while your enemy was busy plotting, they couldn't see you praying and praising. They couldn't see God's plan for their defeat and your victory.

Some Christians are living life all beaten up simply because they won't trust the Lord to fight for them. But He's not going to take the battle from you. You have to give it to Him, like Jehoshaphat did. When he reminded the Lord, "God, these are your people," it wasn't because God needed to be reminded of who He was and what He had done for His people. God knew all of that. But in the process of praying these things to God, Jehoshaphat was giving the battle over to the Lord. Some people are holding on to situations that they need to let go of. The road to victory is prayer, promise, and praise.

Every believer will come upon times when they have to face intense battles that seem sure to bring defeat. When you come to that point in life, just imagine God talking to you, saying, "Look around you. Have I ever abandoned you? Do you not have all that you own because I have blessed you?" And that's the promise you can trust!! When God asks such a question, who can respond negatively? When you trust in Him to fight your battles, you gain an overwhelming sense of peace and outright joy. You can trust that the situation is taken care of. You don't know how, and you don't need to, because it isn't your battle anymore. It is the Lord's.

Have you ever danced and shouted in praise to God all by yourself because you just knew? When you trust in God's promises, you can sing and shout the victory before it even happens. When the battle is the Lord's, you already know how it's going to turn out because God doesn't lose.

As you grow in Christ, you learn that with each battle, through each difficulty, the battle is fought and won while you're on your knees. For everything you need, for every trial and tribulation that you face, the battleground is on your knees. The road to victory is prayer, promise, and praise.

And as for the homeless woman I saw on CNN, as I watched the telecast I prayed for her and her family, I remember praying, "Lord, you've got to find a home for this woman and her children. You've got to do it because this woman has shown her faithfulness to you, even when there is no physical evidence. Surely she has prayed for a home. Through her praise she has put Your Word on the line and You don't break Your Word. This woman is praising You because she's standing on Your promises and You're a God who can't go back on a promise. So now You've got to do it." I never found out the outcome of the woman's story, but I'm confident that God fought her battle and found a home for her and her children. Although I don't know the woman's fate for certain, I am certain that God takes care of His faithful. There are too many witnesses to that truth.

A young minister once told me how he was preparing move his wife and child to the Chicago area so that he could attend seminary. He had been given a scholarship and they had practically everything they needed, but he was exactly $200 short of what he needed for school. Still, he decided to pack his family and their belongings in their van and head north. As they made their way from the South, they had to go through the town where his grandmother lived, so they stopped to visit. As much as he enjoyed seeing his grandmother, his mind was distracted regarding the money he still needed. He couldn't ask his grandmother, who was not able to give him any financial assistance.

While they were there, his grandmother asked him to go to the grocery store to pick up a couple of items. While he was in the grocery store, he ran into a woman who had known him since he was a boy. As they were catching up on old times, the women interjected, "I don't know why, but God is telling me to give you this." The woman proceeded to write a check and give it to him. Without looking at the check, the young minister thanked her for her kindness, and they soon went their separate ways. When he got back to his grandmother's house, he looked at the check—it was written for exactly $200!

Whether you are trusting God for something that seems trivial or for something that seems absolutely overwhelming, always affirm that God is able. As He told Abraham and Sarah, "Is any thing too hard for the LORD?" (Gen. 18:14, KJV). God proclaimed to the great prophet "Jeremiah, Behold, I am the LORD, the God of all flesh: is there any thing too hard for me?" (Jer. 32:27, KJV). The angel Gabriel told young Mary, "For with God nothing shall be impossible" (Luke 1:37, KJV).

We serve a God for whom nothing is too hard, a God who can do anything. Therefore we must never stop praying to the God who is able to do all things.

▲ If you're looking for a better job, don't hit the want ads first; first hit your knees and then praise Him for the job He's already earmarked for you

▲ If you want to be free from the people who are disturbing the peace in your life, don't start fussing and thinking of revenge; get on your knees and then praise God for moving you up to a higher plane.

▲ If you want to find the right man or woman for you, don't hit the club, hit your knees and then praise God for the godly husband or wife He has in mind for you.

▲ If you're waiting for peace to be restored in your home, don't hit the telephone—calling everybody in the family; first hit your knees, and then praise God for your family, a happy, peace-loving family.

Jesus is an equal opportunity General. He'll fight your battles, just like He fought Judah's. If you don't want to go through another day of life trying to fight in your own strength, enlist in His army. Let Him fight your battles if you're tired and battle weary from trying to fight all alone. Let Him lead you down the sure road to victory.

KNOW THE SURE ROAD TO VICTORY
Questions

1. Recall a time when you were under spiritual attack. Did you immediately turn to God or did you attempt to fix the problem yourself? If you turned to God right away, how did God manifest His power and authority to protect and defend you against attack? If you tried to fix it yourself, how did you come to understand that you needed God's help?

2. Why is it impossible to use natural weapons to fight a spiritual enemy?

3. Why is prayer the best action for a believer to start with, whether the battle is spiritual or physical?

4. Why are prayer and fasting considered acts of obedience rather than tools for influencing God? Read Psalm 35:13; Matthew 17:21 (KJV), and Mark 9:29 (KJV).

5. In what ways have God's promises comforted you during difficult periods of your life? Make a list of your favorite Scripture passages, those that you rely on during your times of struggle.

6. Review the points of King Jehoshaphat's prayer. Why do you think he reviewed facts that God already knew? How

does discussing our circumstances help human beings during prayer?

7. The prophet Jahaziel was God's messenger for the promise of victory to Jehoshaphat. How has God used persons in your life to serve as messengers to deliver words of hope and promise to you?

8. Why do you think it was necessary for Jehoshaphat and his army to take their place on the battlefield, even though God had already told them the victory was theirs. When you face problems, do you stand in faith, ready to do battle?

9. Why does standing in faith often prove more challenging and more difficult than acting on our own?

10. Can you praise God for victory in your life even before the victory manifests itself? How do you think God feels when we praise Him before He even responds to our need?

CHAPTER EIGHT

Remember, Things Are Not Always As They Appear

— THE BOOK OF OBADIAH —

THE BOOK OF Obadiah, the shortest book in the Bible with only 21 verses, has several themes, all of which center on the nation of Edom's assistance in the destruction of the nation of Israel. Edom and Israel were first cousins, but they were feuding relatives. Just like the legendary feud between the Hatfields and the McCoys, this rift between Israel and Edom was one between relatives that had continued through the generations.

Much of Obadiah's stern words of prophecy deal with Edom, a nation located south of Judah. The Edomites were the descendants of Esau, the brother of Jacob. The Israelites were the descendants of Jacob. Esau and Jacob were the twin sons of Isaac, the son of Abraham, and the two were in perpetual struggle.

We read in the Book of Genesis that even before they were born, the brothers struggled in their mother's womb. Their antipathy continued throughout their lives, and, consequently, the lives of their descendants—the two nations of Israel and Edom. The two groups of people were not good neighbors. They were not friendly relatives. The descendants of the two brothers had carried on the conflict, which came to a focus in the prophecy of Obadiah. While Jacob and Esau eventually settled their differences, their descendants certainly did not.

For years, their feuding had gone back and forth—and both nations were to blame for the poor relationship that existed between them. The Old Testament contains a number of references to their deliberate efforts to fuel the fires of hostility.

▲ Numbers 20:14–21 records that Edom had refused to allow Moses and the Israelites permission to pass through their land on their way to Canaan.

▲ In Deuteronomy 23:7 (NIV), God instructed the Israelites, "Do not abhor the Edomite, for he is your brother." Yet King David went to war against them anyway, subjugated the Edomites, and imposed governors on them (2 Samuel 8:13-14 and 1 Chronicles 18:12-13).

▲ Sometime later, during the reign of Jehoram, the Edomites rebelled against the domination of Judah (2 Kings 8:20-22) in their land and established their own king.

▲ After the destruction of Judah and the razing of Jerusalem by the Babylonian army, Edom took advantage of the Israelites' vulnerability in their exile. Facing pressure from Arabian tribes from the southern deserts, a group of Edomites invaded much of southern Judah.

Israel's own relatives were rejoicing and actively participating in her destruction. After Israel has been put into exile, essentially kicked out of the Promised Land, the people of Edom were rejoicing over her downfall.

Obadiah addressed this feud between the two nations and delivered a blistering attack on both parties; however, the nation of Edom was the main party addressed here because of its continuing reproach and uncanny ability to kick "cousin" Israel while she is down.

BE CAREFUL HOW YOU TREAT PEOPLE—
ESPECIALLY GOD'S PEOPLE

Do you have a relative—a sibling, cousin, aunt, uncle, or an in-law—who seems to take delight in trying to push you down further? It hurts when any person tries to hurt you while you're down, but it's even worse when that the person is related to you.

Although it's a painful thing to realize, the reality is that in life there are people who are just waiting for you to fall. There are people who are happy when you fall on hard times. In life there are some people who just seem to rejoice at your sorrow.

▲ They don't like it because you strive hard to live in a way that pleases God and can't wait for you to stumble.

▲ They don't like it that you go to church and pay your tithe faithfully.

▲ They don't like it that you study God's Word, attend Bible study and Sunday school and can always draw find comfort in God's Word when you have troubles.

▲ They don't like it that God has blessed you with a new house, a new relationship, a happy marriage, a new job, a few extra dollars in the bank, or a new car.

▲ They don't like it that your children are well adjusted and doing well in school.

In general, they're just mad that things are going well for you and can't wait for something to go wrong. It doesn't matter to them that you may have worked hard to accomplish the things that you have. It doesn't matter to them that you have endured tests and trials faithfully and have been blessed because you've overcome. They're just made because you're blessed and you know it.

At the time of Obadiah's prophecy, the Israelites already had been placed in exile. The people of Edom had gloated and even rejoiced over "cousin" Israel's sorrow. Edom delighted to see Israel pulled down. The Edomites probably thought that the Israelites thought too much of themselves and had taken that "God's chosen" thing just a bit too far. Edom had nursed its grudge against Israel through the years and had refused to let the past stay in the past. Terrible things happen when people can't let go of the past. People who don't let go may think they're doing something to harm the other person when they keep dwelling on the past; but in reality, only the person clinging to past resentments and hurts is the one left hurting. Hanging on to the past only hurts your own spiritual growth and development.

Edom refused to let go of the past and refused to acknowledge Israel as kin. And when destruction came to Israel, Edom rejoiced, even participated in Israel's downfall. Perhaps their adversarial relationship was not rooted in the resentment of Esau, but in the ill feelings that had festered and intensified down through the generations. The Edomites may have felt cheated. They may have thought that if Jacob hadn't stolen Esau's birthright, Edom might have become God's chosen people.

Edom probably didn't like the fact that Israel had a special place in God's heart and promise. The Edomites probably had accused the Israelites of thinking they were better than them. Edom rejoiced over Israel's troubles because that must have been proof that they were not a special people.

People rejoice over the troubles of Christians. Just because you pray, work hard, tithe, and try to live righteously, it does not mean that you won't have trouble. But when people see you experiencing difficulties, it is confirmation for them. They may think, "Well, she ain't nobody special. She has more troubles than I do."

In reality, the facts related to Israel and Edom probably had been distorted over the years. Resentment thrives among families today—often over an issue that no one can accurately identify. The story gets twisted over the years and important facts are omitted as time goes on. Eventually, the story recalled has nothing to do with the truth does little more than affirm the injustice done to the clan that was "wronged."

The part of Israel's story that didn't get told was the fact that God already had determined that Esau would serve Jacob. Rebecca didn't have to trick her husband and cheat her son in order to give her other son Jacob the birthright. But down through the years, Edom's resentment grew. They forgot what God had decided and chose instead to focus on what they felt had been taken away from them. But despite their resentments, Jacob's descendants would become the chosen nation.

Edom's participation in the demise of Israel was both passive and active. It was partially passive because they did nothing to prevent the destruction of Jerusalem. They refused to help the Israelites knowing they were in need. They stood aloof while strangers pillaged the city and murdered its inhabitants. And because they did nothing to prevent the destruction, because they would not lift a finger to help, they were declared to be as bad as those who had actually brought down the walls. Often we pray about sins of commission and sins of omission. Sins of commission are those things we do deliberately in violation of God's law. The sins of omission, however, are the sins we commit through active resistance or neglect of God's law. God said that Edom was just as guilty as any of Israel's enemies because of what they had not done. Edom's sin was a sin of omission, but their hatred of Israel was so intense that their sin was also one of commission.

Edom's participation in Israel's woes was active as well. They deliberately sinned against their neighbor nation. After the destruction of Jerusalem was complete and the Israelites were in exile, the Edomites exploited the situation for their own gain. They rejoiced in the downfall of their cousins because it meant prosperity for themselves. People will talk about you for what you have, but just wait until you don't have it anymore—they'll be in line to get it! Many of us experienced a time in high school when a friend convinced us that the object of our affection was not worth our time. Perhaps a girlfriend said, "He ain't that cute. He doesn't even have a car and he doesn't dress right." But later on, that same girl who was criticizing him was trying to date him!

Israel had been on top during the days of Kings David and Solomon. But by the time of Obadiah, they had been thrown out of the Promised Land, dragged into exile by the army of Babylon, and those left behind were a mere handful of peasants. And Edomites were happy about it.

Here's the big issue. While Israel was facing the consequences of its unfaithfulness to God, what were the Edomites doing? This very question gets at the heart of the Book of Obadiah. Certainly Edom had done bad things by not being a good neighbor and by not being a good relative. But that was not the worse thing they had done. Edom's grave mistake was that they had written off God. And they had written off His people. What Edom did was take advantage of the situation and act like God couldn't do anything about it. They watched Israel's calamity and they rubbed salt into their wounds because they acted like Israel's God was nowhere to be found.

People need to be careful about trying to predict where God is or is not going to move. They need to be careful about writing God off in the life of one of His children. Just when people think God has forgotten about you, that's when God is up to something! No matter how bad things get, and things had gotten pretty bad for Israel, God does not forget His people. God does not leave His people without hope for redemption or change.

Edom had written God off, and because they had written God off, God had to show them something.

YOU'RE NOT TOO BIG TO BE BROUGHT DOWN

Obadiah makes mention in verse 3 that the Edomites live "in the clefts of the rocks" (NIV). The capital of Edom was built high in the mountains. It is a marvel of ancient engineering: it starts with a narrow cavern in the rock, and opens into a space where temples have been carved out from the rock cliff with doorways measuring thirty feet high.

Edom wasn't a large nation, but it was a well-defended nation. The only way into the capitol city was through that narrow cavern in the rock. So even if a nation were to bring an army of thousands against the city, they would be forced to enter almost single file because the entrance was so narrow.

From the references in verses 8 and 9, it seems that the people of Edom were very proud of their military might and their military strategists. They were well defended both by natural and by human resources. The inhabitants felt secure; yet God was about to humble them. There is no lasting security apart from God. So, for Edom things were not as they appeared. The story wasn't over because God was about to step in.

As America is considered the world's leading superpower, most Americans thought the nation was impenetrable and invulnerable. However, on September 11, 2001, our nation discovered that we are not inviolable, as we once believed. We thought that because we have a large military budget, the latest technology, and seemingly unlimited resources, no nation or enemy would dare to attack us. But we were wrong. No fortress is impenetrable. No situation, person, or condition is totally invulnerable. So for those seeking guarantees from trouble in the Christian faith, remember that no matter how much you pray and praise God, you are still vulnerable. No matter how much you go to church or how faithfully you pay your tithe, you are not invincible. Because believers are human, we remain vulnerable to attack from Satan.

No matter how strong and self-sufficient we appear, we are vulnerable to attack. We may appear self-sufficient when we think we can make our own decisions regarding our friends and acquaintances, where we go to school, who we marry, what career we pursue, or where we live. We think nothing can touch us when we have a few extra dollars in the bank, when we think we have job security or marriage guarantees. In other words, when we think we're in charge, we're relying on our limited human wisdom and talent, not in the power of God. This was the faulty attitude of Edom: "We're large and in charge." In verse 8, God says He will "destroy the wise men of Edom" (NIV). Israel had to deal with the consequences of their disobedience, but Edom had a much higher price to pay. God basically said, in verse 4 "You're flying high as an eagle right now, but I'm going to bring you down." God was telling them, "Things are not as they appear. I'm going to bring you down."

It's a terrible thing when God says "I will bring you down." First, it's bad because you know it's going to happen if God says that it will. Second, since God has all power, you don't know the level of force He will use to bring you down. It's a terrible thing to be on God's hit list!

Edom had done some terrible things by failing to support Israel and actively contributing to her destruction. The Lord declared that it was Edom's pride that would cause her own ruin. "The pride of your heart has deceived you" (v. 3, NIV). And although Edom thought that the nation was impenetrable, unassailable, and inviolable, God said that they would be brought low. They would come crashing down to the earth. The Book of Proverbs says, "Pride goeth before destruction, and an haughty spirit before a fall" (16:18, KJV).

DON'T COUNT GOD OUT

Edom had watched Israel's calamity, and they had rubbed salt into Israel's wounds. The trouble was that Edom had written off God a bit too quickly. They had decided that Israel was finished for good, but things were not as they appeared. And for that, Edom was going to pay the consequences. Because what Edom didn't realize was that the exile of the Israelites wasn't God's last word on the subject.

Sometimes when you experience trouble, it's important to remember that things are not as they appear because God always has the last word.

▲ If you're threatened with losing your job, remember that God has the last word.

▲ If you see someone you love being influenced by the wrong people to do the wrong thing, remember that God has the last word.

▲ If you're troubled about a situation that just doesn't look like it's going to end in your favor, remember that God has the last word.

▲ When it seems like the wicked continue to prosper, and that people can do anything to anyone and never suffer the consequences of the pain they inflict, remember that God has the last word.

▲ More important, if God has made you a promise, and it just doesn't seem like it's going to happen, take hope in the fact that God has the last word.

Regarding Israel, God had made big promises to them—starting with Abraham. He had big plans for His people and for His kingdom. And He's still not finished yet with His plans for His people to this day. Israel had been punished for their disobedience to God, and Edom was rejoicing—but the story was not over. Things were not as they appeared—not for Israel nor for Edom.

While the people of Israel were experiencing the trauma and shame of losing their homeland, the Edomites had been sitting on the sidelines gloating over how their archrival had been wiped out. They were smiling in their confidence that Edom was left standing as the stronger of the two nations. But they had spoken too soon. Things were not as they appeared.

Playing a game of "Who's the strongest?" can be both dangerous and deceptive. On December 1, 1955, an unknown black seamstress in Montgomery, Alabama refused to give up her seat on the bus to a white passenger. Those in power arrested her because they thought that they were in charge. But things were not as they appeared. After her arrest, a small band of black folks, with no political or economic power, managed to bring down an entire city transportation system. Things were not as they appeared.

In the 1962 system of apartheid in South Africa, a member of the rebel African National Congress (ANC) named Nelson Mandela was arrested for leaving the country illegally and inciting a riot among the blacks of the nation. He was sentenced to life imprisonment. The government thought they were silencing Mandela for life. But things were not as they appeared. What they actually were doing was bringing worldwide attention to the problem of apartheid in South Africa. By putting Mandela in prison, the South African government actually brought more attention to him! Things were not as they appeared.

In 1963, four little girls were killed right after Sunday school when a bomb exploded in the basement of a Birmingham church. Local Ku Klux Klan members thought they were teaching the local blacks a lesson and that the result would be frightened silence. But things were not as they appeared. What those Klansmen did by bombing that church was let the world know and shame our nation into admitting that—yes—there is a vicious and deeply rooted race problem in America.

You may recall a circumstance when someone you know was on top—living large and in charge—but all of a sudden, things changed. Things were not as they appeared. I remember a friend recalling her selection as a high school debutante, sponsored by the local chapter of a sorority. She couldn't understand why she was chosen instead of a young lady who was a member of a prominent local family. Things were not as they appeared. It later became known that the young lady, though from a prominent family, was engaging in activities that were unbecoming. Meanwhile, my friend, the daughter of a poor family with no social standing, was chosen for the honor.

Perhaps you know someone from high school, college, or your younger years who didn't turn out quite the way you would have thought because things were not as they appeared. Maybe the young man voted "most likely to succeed" in high school ended up strung out on crack. Maybe the young lady who was most popular actually had very low self-esteem because of years of sexual abuse she endured at home. Circumstances cannot always be assessed by their appearance. Perhaps you remember the guy who could "pull" all the women because he had a clean ride and clean threads. Meanwhile, you were a struggling college student who had no car and few clothes. Where is he today? Where are you today?

Obadiah said to the Edomites in verse 15 that the day of the Lord was near for all nations: "As you have done, it will be done to you; your deeds will return upon your own head" (NIV). God was telling them, "Just like you drank and partied in your victory on my holy hill, just like you celebrated the fall of Jerusalem, the nations will drink and drink, until finally there's nothing left." God was telling Edom, "What goes around comes around."

The Edomites would have to face the consequences of their sins of omission and commission. And in the end, all the nations who looked so strong, all the voices that poured scorn on Israel, every kingdom, would be gone. Singer Jerry Butler had a hit song titled, "Only the Strong Survive." And indeed that's true. The trouble is, the one who appears mightiest isn't necessarily the strongest. Not long after I moved into my home, a neighbor gave me two dogwood trees that he dug up from his yard. Almost immediately, one tree appeared strong and vibrant, budding during its first year. The other appeared weak, giving no hint of life that first spring. By the next spring, the tree that appeared strong and healthy was dead and the tree that appeared weak is still blossoming year after year. Things were not as they appeared. The tree that appeared strongest did not survive the long haul.

Since we operate in two worlds, both spiritual and temporal, we recognize that things are not always as they appear. You can't count God out. Whenever someone tries to make life hard for you, remember that things are not as they appear because God Almighty has the last word. Whenever you feel like you are the underdog because you have obeyed God, remember that things are not always as they appear.

▲ When you face trials and tribulations, don't count God out.

▲ Other people may be eagerly anticipating your downfall, but don't count God out.

▲ Maybe God blessed you with a house and now you're having a little trouble paying the note. While some people are waiting for you to lose the house, you need to tell them, "Don't count God out."

▲ Maybe you're back in church, but having more trouble at home than ever before. Don't count God out.

▲ Maybe you have a dream that keeps running into roadblocks. Don't count God out.

▲ Hebrews 11:1 (KJV) says "Faith is the substance of things hoped for, the evidence of things not seen." Don't count God out. Things are not as they appear. It ain't over 'til it's over.

There is a reason why we who live in the temporal world but operate in the spiritual can live in the confidence that things are not always as they appear.

GOD KEEPS HIS WORD

God keeps His Word to bless His faithful. I am forever reminded that the life of my parents is a lasting testimony that God rewards faithfulness. They were able to put four children through college on a preacher's paycheck. Like the story about the bumble bee that can fly although it's impossible from an aerodynamic perspective, my parents providing their children to obtain higher education was humanly improbable but God made it possible. As they managed to somehow find tuition money out of a pastor's salary, there were people in our town who made much more money than my parents but they were unable to provide the same benefit for their children. Things are not always as they appear.

God had made a promise that through Abraham's line He would build a kingdom that would bring blessings to the entire world. He promised Abraham in Genesis 12:3 (NIV), "I will bless those who bless you and whoever curses you I will curse; and all peoples on earth will be blessed through you." And for Obadiah, no matter how bad things looked, no matter how great Israel's mistakes or how much the people had been made to suffer their consequences of her disobedience to God, His promise to His people was still standing.

And that's how the shortest book in the Old Testament closes. Edom had been gloating because it looked like Israel had had it. Edom had been cursing the people God had promised to bless. But the tables were going to be turned. Edom, who was on top, would end up with nothing. But the kingdom of God will flourish. Even today, thousands of years later, millions of people flock to Jerusalem and Israel each year to see that wonderful city. Many times you've heard someone say, "I'm going to visit Israel or Jerusalem." How many times have you heard someone say, "I'm going to visit Edom"? Few people today know where Edom is, but they once surpassed Israel in recognition and infamy!

No matter how bad things look, no matter how much other people gloat and rejoice in your troubles, God's people can stand firm in the fact that God honors His promises. It doesn't matter what things look like. Things are not what they appear.

Jesus' first public sermon was "the kingdom of God is at hand" (Matt. 4:17, NIV). True to God's promise, the Deliverer has come through the line of David, except that Jesus brought deliverance in a most unexpected way. Jesus' kingdom doesn't look like much when viewed with human eyes because His kingdom is made up of ordinary people who have taken Jesus as their King. His is a kingdom that people may laugh at and mock, just like the Edomites mocked Israel.

On the outside, God's people may not look like much, but God's people are not to be messed with! Things are not what they appear.

Some people delight in seeing Christians face tough times, and some people want to believe that following Christ is a thing of the past. They think that it's old fashioned or out-of-style. But the truth is exactly the opposite. Christians are people of the future, and our future is absolutely guaranteed because God keeps His Word. The body of Christ may not look like much to the world, but take heart—things are not what they appear!

Obadiah got it right. He told the Edomites, "You can laugh. You can mock. But God's Kingdom is going to stand forever. It's still going to be there when you're long gone. He was right then and he's still right today. Although we may not look like much to the world, even the most humble, most lowly Christian is going to be in heaven for eternity. Long after the powers of this world are gone, God's people will still be around, celebrating in God's kingdom because God keeps His Word.

The next time you're facing a hard time for your faith, the next time someone laughs or tries to ridicule you for being a child of God, the next time you're tempted to just give up because it's tough, the next time you're caught up in the things that threaten to drag you away from God, remember that things are not what they appear. There's only one Kingdom that's going to last.

REMEMBER, THINGS ARE NOT ALWAYS AS THEY APPEAR

Questions

1. Why do you think people continue to hold grudges, resentment, and hatred, even when the issue has long since passed or even after several generations have passed?

2. Have you ever secretly rejoiced at someone else's downfall? How do you feel when someone rejoices over your downfall?

3. Why must people, both believers and unbelievers alike, be careful how they treat God's people?

4. Why do you think some people lie in wait for things to go wrong in the lives of others?

5. Why is it important for people to let go of the past? What happens to people who continue to nurse grudges and hold on to old issues?

6. Recall a time in your life when you remained confident in faith that things were not as they appeared. How did God reveal His authority over all things, even if it appeared for a time that the enemy would win?

7. Why do you think some people "write God off" when He seems slow to act in a situation?

8. Have you ever known someone who seemed to feel as though he or she was too big to be brought down? How does God humble those who are filled with false pride?

9. Why has a proud heart been the downfall of so many men and women, Christians and non-Christians alike?

10. Why is it important that we never count God out?

11. Why is Israel's experience with Edom a reminder to us today to maintain faith in God, as things are not always what they appear?

12. Why do some people rejoice when Christians face tough times?

CHAPTER NINE

Never Forget Who You Are

— MATTHEW 10:16-23 —

IN THIS PASSAGE, Jesus is speaking a message of both warning and encouragement to his disciples. He warns them that they will face hostilities and persecutions for His sake. Yet He gave them a promise: Those who stand firm till the end will be saved" (Matt. 10:22, NIV). In other words He was telling them not to stop—no matter what!

If ever a person was looking for a reason not to become a disciple of Jesus Christ, it certainly can be found in Matthew 10:16-23. If there ever was a training course on how not to recruit volunteers or how not to sell a product, this passage has got to be it. Jesus gathered His disciples and told them in no uncertain terms what it would be like if they followed Him, if they went out into the world and bore the name Christian. A lot of people come to Jesus because of what they hope He can do for them. They don't think about what it is going to cost them. Salvation is free, but discipleship is costly.

In this passage, Jesus talked to them about the persecution, suffering, broken relationships, and even death they would face if they decided to follow Him. Why did Jesus tell them this? Was He trying to scare them off? No, Jesus is always ready to welcome disciples into the fold. Jesus told them this because He was a realist. He knew that the world His disciples live in, then and now, is not very friendly to Christians. It's a very friendly to Christian who are talking to other Christians, or even other religious people. You can talk about Jesus at church, or even at a local family restaurant, but if you dare go to a nightclub to talk about Jesus and tell somebody they need to be saved, they'll turn on you like wolves!

Jesus was sending His disciples out to do missions—His work. It's reasonable to assume that God Incarnate knew that when His disciples faced these kinds of pressures, having gone into a hostile world, they would be tempted to forget who they were and deny their identity as Christians.

It's been over twenty-five years since the mini-series "Roots" aired on CBS for the first time. In one of the early episodes, the young African warrior Kunte Kinte was purchased by a plantation owner in Annapolis, Maryland and was put to work in the field. Kunte Kinte's new owner decided he was going to change his new slave's name to Toby—something that was more pleasing to the master's Eurocentric sensibilities.

Slavery is not just about physical bondage; it's about mental bondage, too. Conventional wisdom regarding slavery dictated that the slave owner had to keep the slave bound in mind as well as body. That's one reason why it was illegal to teach a slave how to read or write. Reading is the key to knowledge and knowledge is power. One of the other common practices of slavery in America was to cut the slaves off from their homeland by not allowing them to retain their culture, punishing them for using their native language, forbidding their to practice their religion, and changing their African names to something that sounded more familiar to the master.

That is why it was so important for Kunte Kinte's master to change his new slave's name. But at first, when Kunte Kinte was called Toby, he didn't respond. He was a proud African—proud of his name, one of his last connections to his past.

When he was first called Toby, his only reply was "My name Kunte Kinte." That's when the overseer decided to break the African down so that he would adopt his slave name. The overseer tied the young African to a post and asked him, "What is your name?" Kunte replied defiantly, "My name Kunte...Kunte Kinte." And then "Crack!" The whip ripped into Kunte flesh. Again the overseer asked, "What is you name?" Hurt, but with some fight in him, Kunte repeats his African name. Again the whip began to pierce open Kunte back. His flesh begins to bleed and burn. Repeatedly he is asked, "What is your name?" And repeatedly Kunte replies, "My name Kunte Kinte." Kunte was beaten until his back looked like a brown patchwork quilt.

Finally, when Kunte Kinte seemed to be near death, the overseer again asked, "What's your name?" Barely able to speak, the proud young African mutters. "Toby." As if to humiliate him and beat him down further, the overseer commanded him to repeat his slave name. Kunte, in a broken voice with tears and sweat pouring down his face replied, "My name Toby."

There's something wrapped up in our names isn't there? Our names identify us and sometimes even our sense of purpose. Kunte Kinte's name symbolized his culture and his heritage. It was all that he had left of the homeland and the life he had loved. Our names are all about who we are, our character and personality; our names define us.

That was even more the case in Jesus' day when one's name really did express what kind of character or personality or life mission a person had. The name Elijah means "the Lord is God." The name Elisha means "the Lord is salvation." The name Jabez means "pain" or "sorrow." And since the time of the twelve disciples, every person who has decided to join with Christ takes upon himself or herself the new name that He gives us when we surrender our lives to Him. That name is "Christian."

Christians are just like Abram whose name was changed to Abraham, or like Jacob whose name was changed to Israel, or Simon whose name was changed to Peter. Those followers of God had had genuine, life-changing experiences with the Almighty. And those who are Christians today have met that same Christ. If we really have met Him, then He has changed us. And if we let Him lead us, He will transform us—right down to our name. One of my coworkers was looking at a picture of a local pastor and commented, "I never thought that she would become a minister." But God takes our lives and makes us what He would have us to be. That's the danger of letting Christ lead us. When He leads, we lose the ability to control where we are going. Abraham didn't know where he was going when the Lord called him. Read Jeremiah 29:11 (NIV): "'For I know the plans I have for you,'" declares the LORD, "'plans to prosper you and not to harm you, plans to give you hope and a future.'" When we put our lives in God's hands, we may not know where we are going but we know that we cannot fail.

Jesus tells those of us who bear the precious name of Christian that we're called to go out into the world and we're going to be like lambs in the midst of wolves. The world is like a wolf in its attitude toward those who have made Jesus Christ the center of their lives. The world growls, "Who are you?" And we say, "We're lambs." The wolves that threaten attack are not those in the woods. They are not wolves like the one that was after Little Red Riding Hood. These wolves are demons of sarcasm, criticism, jealousy, envy, corruption, hopelessness, oppression, despair, economic pressure, and doubt—these are the wolves that threaten to tear Christians apart.

We see all the things going on in the world and the wolves begin to attack us because we have chosen to serve Jesus Christ; we stop and we count the cost. We may ask ourselves, "Is this worth it?" And after you've asked yourself the question, you may be tempted to forget your name. You may be tempted to deny who you really are. And the wolves of revenge and retaliation, of materialism, of immorality, of gossip and slander, and of dishonesty gather and encircle believers and try to make us forget our name. At our weakest moment they ask us "What's your name?" Sometimes, sounding as weak as Kunte Kinte after his beating, we reply weakly, "Christian." There are times when we may feel to weak to respond boldly in the faith. We feel too weak to stand up for Jesus because Satan is doing a job on us—attacking us on the job, attacking us in our homes, attacking our finances, even attacking us at church. A serious wolf attack can beat you down.

When we're in church among our Christian friends, we can say loud and strong, "I'm a Christian! I love the Lord!" But after church is over and the wolves have chased us around and beat us down, we are tempted to forget who we are. When we stand up and say, "My name is Christian," they respond, "No, your name is Sinner." They tell you that your name is Sinner because they want you to fall back into spiritual bondage. They want you to be a slave to sin, to fear, to anger, to immorality, to revenge, and to unforgiveness.

On the surface, it may seem that if you want to get somewhere at work, be accepted in school, get a date, or not look unacceptable to the people around you, life may seem a whole lot easier if you say, "My name Sinner" and give in to spiritual bondage. Some Christians deny who they are called to be because of the pressures that surround them.

But we can't say that He didn't warn us. Jesus said, "They will hand you over to the local councils and flog you in their synagogues" (Matt. 10:17, NIV). In other words, "It can get so bad out there that even your friends and your family may turn on you if you really place your allegiance with Me." And when we hear that we may say to ourselves, "Hmm, maybe there is another way to do this." In our hearts, all Christians want to serve Jesus. We want to go wherever He calls us to go and do whatever He calls us to do. But at the same time, nobody wants to be persecuted, oppressed, mistreated, talked about, or lied on—not even for Jesus! So we are tempted to forget who we are and deny our name.

What are the trials and temptations in your life that are pressing on you right now? What wolves are circling around you, tempting you to forget who you are?

▲ Maybe it's the temptation to cheat or steal for temporary monetary gain.

▲ Maybe it's buying expensive clothes that are hot, or maybe it shoplifting, because you feel the need to impress somebody.

▲ Maybe it's substance abuse; you're afraid you'll die without it.

▲ Maybe it's a relationship that you know is unhealthy, but your self-esteem is so low that you're afraid to leave.

▲ Maybe it's refusing to encourage someone so that you can feel better about yourself.

▲ Maybe you're tempted to turn your back on justice or wrongdoing because you've convinced yourself that it's none of your business.

▲ Maybe you're telling yourself that you can't help anybody else because you need help yourself.

▲ Maybe you're tempted to ignore God's call on your life because of what other people might say.

Maybe you're tempted to be a closet Christian at certain times. There may be times when you don't think it's expedient to reveal your faith. You want to identify with the masses, with the world. You find it easier to say, "My name Toby." That way, you don't go through all the ridicule, persecution, criticism and harassment that comes with really living unashamedly as a sold-out servant of Jesus Christ.

We're not alone when we feel the temptation to forget our name. There in that courtyard on the eve of Jesus' crucifixion, Peter denied knowing Jesus three times and in so doing denied his own name. We in the Christian community tend to give Peter a lot of grief for that, don't we? Truthfully, I wish that, at the end of my life, I could say that I've denied Jesus only three times. How many times have you denied Christ by your actions? How many times have you denied knowing Jesus because of your sinful behavior? How many times have you denied knowing Jesus because you refused to give in support of the Kingdom? How many times have you denied knowing Jesus because you craved social acceptance? The pressures that Jesus warned His disciples about are always present.

Whether you're a missionary, a preacher/pastor, a deacon, a Sunday school teacher, a trustee, an usher, a choir member, a youth worker, or a pew warmer, being a Christian is no piece of cake. If it's done right, it's always about sacrifice. A missionary doesn't always feel like telling the world about Jesus when the people are hostile to hearing it. The Sunday school teacher doesn't always want to take the high road. The preacher doesn't always want to be a pastor trying to help members to quit claiming the name Toby.

Whatever we are called to do, we must do it in Jesus' name. We cannot deny Christ because Christ did not deny us. Bearing His name is a privilege. No matter what comes, we have to continue to stand and to claim Him. God will fight your battles. He will let the wolves of the world know your name, and thereby let them know what His name is. And in so doing, He gives you the power to stand.

On February 6, 1967, heavyweight champion Muhammad Ali fought a bout against Ernie Terrell. Prior to the fight, Terrell had refused to call Ali by his Muslim name—a ploy that infuriated Ali—choosing instead to call him Cassius Clay. Ali, amid the swirling controversy associated with his conversion to Islam and his draft status, was in no mood for Ernie Terrell or anyone else to be messing with him about his name. Ali had been quoted as saying, "Cassius Clay is a slave name. I didn't choose it, and I didn't want it. I am Muhammad Ali, a free name—it means 'beloved of God'—and I insist people use it when speaking to me and of me."

When the two men got in the ring, it was obvious that Terrell could not beat Ali, but he did manage to last for the duration of the fight, something no other fighter had done at the time. By the end of round fifteen, however, Terrell's eyes were swollen shut, and he had suffered a serious beat down at the hands of Ali.

During the fight, using a chilling combination of brutality and skill, Ali pummeled Terrell, repeatedly chanting, "What's my name?" With each succeeding flurry of punches Ali screamed at his opponent, "What's my name? And, as only "The Greatest of All Time" could say, young, cocky Ali repeatedly asked Terrell, "What's my name, Fool? What's my name?"

And so it is with God dealing with those who refuse to acknowledge the Lord as the Most High God—those who persecute servants who have been sent in His name.

When Moses went to Pharaoh as God's representative, he told the Egyptian king that Yahweh wanted Pharaoh to let His people go. Pharaoh was indignant. He believed himself to be the sole authority of Egypt. Pharaoh asked Moses in

Exodus 5:2 (NIV), "Who is the LORD, that I should obey him and let Israel go? I do not know the LORD and I will not let Israel go."

But through the plagues, God showed Pharaoh who He was then and who He continues to be in the world. With each devastating plague, God was asking Pharaoh: "What's my name, Fool?" And Pharaoh was a fool because the Bible tells us that only a fool says there is no God (Psalm 14:1; 53:1).

▲ God said to Pharaoh, "What's my name?" and the water turned to blood.

▲ God said to Pharaoh, "What's my name?" and frogs take over the land.

▲ God said to Pharaoh, "What's my name?" and darkness covers the sky.

▲ God said to Pharaoh, "What's my name?" and chariot wheels start falling off.

▲ God said to Pharaoh, "What's my name?" and one plague after another comes until finally He asks, "What's my name?" and the first born of Egypt are dead.

By the time the Lord got through doing a beat down on Egypt with those ten plagues, Pharaoh knew Israel's God. He knew that Moses' God was more powerful than his god. The Lord says, "Don't mess with my anointed" (1 Chron. 16:22). There are serious consequences for those who dare attempt to challenge God's followers. Just ask the 450 prophets of Baal who got wiped out at Mount Carmel as Elijah called down fire from heaven (1 Kings 18). The prophet of God was asking them, "What's my name?"

When we claim our true name as Christians, we don't have to worry. Yes, we will experience some difficult and trying times, but if we stick with the Lord, those trials will make us stronger.

When you are among the wolves and they try to crush you with lies and gossip, remember your name. And if the wolves don't watch out, the Lord will step in and ask them, "What's my name?" No mother is going let somebody talk about her child and not defend that child. No father is going to let somebody just beat up on his child. Likewise, God won't let folks just beat up on His children. If you're tempted to put your light under a bushel, don't forget your name. If you're tempted to give in to the wolves, don't forget your name. When people try to keep you from serving God, don't forget your name. When people persecute and abuse you, don't forget who you are. Because, all the while, your Father is standing by ready to tell them, "Now don't make Me have to jump in this." Before you go out among the wolves, you need to be certain of who you are as a child of God.

▲ If you're tempted to put your light under a bushel, don't forget your name.

▲ If you're tempted to give in to the wolves, don't forget your name.

▲ When people try to keep you from serving God, don't forget your name.

▲ When people persecute and abuse you, don't forget your name.

What's in a name? Think about it the next time you're tempted to forget who you are in Christ Jesus. You are a member of the royal family—a child of the King. Don't lay claim to spiritual slavery. There's power in the name of Jesus! The devil will try to make you think that being a slave to sin is better than being a child of God. But the Bible says every that knee shall bow and every tongue shall confess the name of Jesus as Lord (Isaiah 45:23; Romans 14:11; Philippians 2:10-11).

Jesus was saying to His disciples, "Despite your persecutions, those who endure to the end will be saved." It's those who endure to the end, who remember their name and claim that name faithfully—they will experience the salvation of God firsthand. They will sing with integrity and authenticity.

Maybe you're reading this and thinking "That waiting at the end stuff sounds good, but I have a hard enough time trying to make it through 24 hours bearing this name, let alone enduring to the end." But remember that Jesus never gave in, even when Satan tried to tempt Him at His weakest moment in the desert. When we have given in, He hasn't. When we have denied who we are, we must remember that Christ never has denied His Father or His disciples. Even when we have failed and turned our backs on Him, He has never turned His back on us. That is the good news of the Gospel—He will never leave or forsake us.

No matter who you are, no matter what you've done, no matter how many times you've denied your name—and thereby denied Christ, He continually swings the door open to you to return unto Him. And here's more good news: He gives you Power—power to endure whatever comes your way for His sake. That Power is the Holy Spirit.

In 1917, one of history's worst episodes of genocide occurred. Approximately 750,000 Armenian Christians were massacred by Muslim Turks. The Turks lined up the Christians: men, women, boys, and girls. Behind them they dug massive trenches that would be their graves. Then the soldiers gave the Armenian Christians a choice: they went down the line to each person, stuck a revolver under the chin and said, "Mohammed or Christ?" There it was: the name. They had a choice now—choose Mohammed and live or choose Jesus and die. And those who were standing there saw what happened when the person before them said the wrong name—Bam! Yet time after time, boys and girls, men and women, one after another, responded with, "Christ, only Christ." And with one fatal shot, into, one by one into the trench they went. What gave those people, the strength, the power, and the ability to respond like that? Certainly not their own strength. The human instinct is to survive at all costs.

The Holy Spirit is unleashed in the world and we place our life and our death in the hands of Christ, by saying, "I claim the name of Christian; I'm going to bear that name at all costs." Then God says, "I'm going to empower you to keep that vow and I am going to give you my Holy Spirit." The Spirit has given us power to do things that are far beyond our imagination! Some people have never experienced a name change. They've never surrendered to Christ, even though they say, "Oh, but I go to church every Sunday." Going to church doesn't make a person a Christian any more than going to a garage makes someone a mechanic. There's a difference between being religious and being a Christian. Jesus wants to know who you are as you go into the world to represent Him and proudly proclaim your identity. The choice is yours.

NEVER FORGET WHO YOU ARE
Questions

1. List the responsibilities of being a Christian that may cause you to have reservations about doing God's work. How do you think you can overcome those reservations?

2. How has Christ prepared you to do what He has called and purposed for you to do?

3. In what ways have the challenges of life caused you to forget that you are a Christian?

4. In what ways have you lived up to the name of Christian?

5. How has being a Christian changed your life—whether you have been a believer for a short time or for most of your life?

6. Do you believe that God has a purpose for your life? How have you tried to discern that purpose?

7. Have you ever been fearful of letting Christ lead you? How have you been able to move past your fears to allow Him to lead you and fulfill His purpose in you?

8. Have you ever felt that being a Christian is not worth the struggle? If so, how has Christ guided you back to a position of strength and wholeness in Him?

9. Most of us have observed people who lead ungodly lives, yet seem to prosper out of their ungodliness. How can you remain strong in your faith and determination in spite of the inequities of life?

10. Consider a specific instance when God demonstrated His power to defeat those who were aiding the powers of evil to undermine His work—either in you or in someone you know. Pray for strength and renewal in Christ that He will continue to sustain and preserve His people.

11. Recall the ways that God opened the door of forgiveness, even when you denied Him through your disobedience to Him. Offer a prayer of thanksgiving to the Lord for His never-ending openness to extend forgiveness to the penitent.

CHAPTER TEN

Dare to Take Some Risks

— RUTH 1:1-17 —

HAVE YOU ever made a decision that went against common sense, yet you knew God was leading you to do it? For example, while Saul of Tarsus was persecuting Christians and issuing death threats, the apostles were still spreading the Gospel. While Herod Agrippa was plotting how many Christians he could kill, following the execution of John, the Church prayed and Peter slept in his prison cell as he awaited his own fate. In the midst of trials, God expects His people to be faithful to Him.

The story of Ruth, Naomi, and Orpah yields some interesting and insightful lessons about the importance of making the right choices in life. As their story unfolds in the Book of Ruth, these three widowed women were facing some difficult life choices. In those days, two of the few choices a widowed woman had was to go back to her family or to find another husband. The choices that these women made regarding their future can teach all believers a lesson about the importance of acting in faith.

ORPAH (SYMBOL OF THE HUMAN DESIRE FOR SECURITY)

From a very early age, most of us are taught to value security, to do all that we can to plan for the future, save for a rainy day, and so forth. Orpah, like most people, especially a widow during ancient times, believed that security was important. In fact, her mother-in-law clearly valued security as she encouraged her daughters-in-law to go back to their families. Hopefully, there they would find husbands who would secure their futures.

Orpah was a Gentile from the land of Moab. She had been widowed, but she was still young enough to remarry and have children. Orpah had a choice between taking a risk and moving to a foreign land with her in-laws or going back to her family. Initially, Orpah was willing to make the pilgrimage to Israel. She started bravely, but then she allowed herself to be turned around.

In Orpah's defense, the odds did not look good for the three widowed women, one of them an old woman. "Naomi's right," she must have thought. "I would be better off at home with my family. I don't need to go to some foreign land where they may mistreat me because I'm from Moab."

Going back to family was a safe prospect. In this "I gotta think about me!" age, we relate to the understanding that we have to look out for ourselves first. In the days of Orpah, Ruth, and Naomi, marriage was security. Orpah wasn't so much choosing against her in-laws as she was choosing in favor of what she perceived to be a secure future.

Some of us are choosing to stay in our own Moabs because we perceive that it's safe. We all have, or have had, some Moabs in our lives—those false securities and safety nets. We tell ourselves that it's okay to stay there because we're too afraid to make a move. Our Moab may be barren land with no hope of opportunity there. The land may be lacking any sense of challenge, adventure, or fulfillment, but it's safe. Nothing bad is going to happen there, but nothing exciting will happen there either.

There is nothing wrong with having safety nets in life. It's just good sense and good planning to have things that we can fall back on. The problem with our perceived security blankets lies in trusting our safeguards more than we trust God. We err when we trust our common sense more than the leading of the Holy Spirit.

Orpah apparently chose what seemed best to her at the time, so she went back to her family. She probably led a normal, safe, and secure life upon her return. It is reasonable to assume that she remarried, and possibly had children, too. Her choice was safe, but the real adventure was brewing in the lives of her more daring in-laws.

In reality, most people are either afraid to take a risk or they're just too lazy. It was definitely a risky venture for two Moabite women to go to Israel. The truth is that God did not make humankind to be caretakers only, but also risk-takers. God did not create us to live in the comfort zone, but in the sometimes nebulous zone of faith, which means living according to Hebrews 11:1—living in the substance of things hoped for and the evidence of the unseen. Just like a car runs on gasoline and like an appliance runs on electricity, the lives of great men and women run on risk and adventure—that's what makes them great. Historian Arnold Toynbee has observed that adventure has made civilization.

Think about the risk takers who, because of their daring, have influenced our lives. Moses led the children of Israel out of Egypt on an adventure. When Columbus sailed the ocean blue, he was on an adventure to prove that there was a New World yet unseen. The Pilgrims, who risked their lives to come to America, went on an adventure that has since shaped the American attitude that we can tackle anything. The American Revolution was an adventure for our nation's founders against

British rule. Our nation's space exploration program has been an adventure.

This is what makes a civilization great—the willingness to venture out to become greater. This same spirit of adventure makes us great individually. The saddest day in any life is when that individual loses his or her sense of adventure. It is a form of death. So important is the spirit of adventure to life that it has been said that many people die at age 25, but are buried at age 75. Their burial is simply a delayed acknowledgment of the death that took place fifty years earlier. Death is more than the cessation of breathing. It is also the cessation of risk and adventure.

Be careful with the over-utilization of words like comfort and convenience, thinking these things alone define a life blessed by God. Be careful when you begin to lead a conventional, quiet, predictable life that is acceptable to everyone. If you are, then it's time to check the barometer of life and see whether you are really alive or merely existing.

Many if not most human beings have a low tolerance threshold for adventure. The more comfortable we get in life, the less willing we become to be risk-takers. As long as her husband was alive, Orpah probably had a comfortable life. She was in search of more comfort, not risk and adventure—faith-based or otherwise.

But the truth is that those who attempt nothing accomplish nothing. People stay in dead-end jobs because they are secure. Women stay in dead-end relationships that are defined as, "That's my baby's daddy," instead of "That's my husband and my baby's daddy." Men stay in dead-end circumstances because they are unwilling to fight convention. People in general won't take a risk and leave a situation that's going nowhere. Instead, they settle for half a man or half a woman, half a relationship, half a job, and half a life.

People go to a Baskin-Robbins© ice cream parlor, where they have thirty-one different flavors, and order a scoop of vanilla because it's safe and familiar. Some of us are afraid to try one of the other thirty flavors because we might not like them. Some people go to a five-star restaurant featuring filet mignon, pasta al dente, and lobster blended in white wine sauce and order fried chicken. We're afraid to adventure past the familiar because that's all that we know.

The fact of the matter is no one can live without risks. The idea of a risk-free life is an illusion. Where can you go that is without risk? What can you do that does not involve a measure of risk? Whenever you drink water, you run the risk of ingesting bacteria, lead, or mercury contaminants. By eating beef you risk mad cow disease. If you're vegetarian, many fruits and vegetables are sprayed with pollutants and pesticides. Driving is a risk because there are drunk or distracted drivers all around. If you take medications to get well, you run the risk of an allergic reaction. Marriage is a risk and courting means looking for the evidence. But all the evidence doesn't always show up until after marriage. Having children is a risk because they may have birth defects or they may grow up and make you sorry they were ever born. Even breathing air is a risk. All of life is a risk.

Adventure and risk are the way God designed us to accomplish great things because they require us to live in faith. The writer of Psalm 107 took great risks. He witnessed the works of the Lord and the wonders of the Lord in the deep. The same can be said of Abraham, who took a risk at age 75. He packed up everything and headed west. Abraham left, not knowing where his mail could be forwarded. He asked God, "How do I know when I am there?" God responded, "I'll tell you when." But Abraham didn't complain. He didn't argue and he didn't question any further. He just went on a great adventure. What was the result of his risk-taking adventure?

Abraham became the father of two great nations, both Jews and Moslems.

Dr. Anthony Campolo, a media commentator and professor emeritus of sociology at Eastern University, once interviewed fifty people who were age 95 and older. He asked them the question, "What would you do different if you could live your life over again?" Practically all of them said three things: First, I would have invested more in my relationships. Second, I would have taken more risks. Third, I would have invested in more things that will live on after I'm dead.

When friends and loved ones part company, they often say to each other, "Take care." This well-intended expression communicates endearment, concern, and support. But pause for a moment to imagine how differently you might have developed if caring people in your family had frequently affirmed to you, "Take risks!" instead of "Take care," as you walked away. How different would you be today if the people in your social circles would encourage you to take risks, instead of cautioning you to take care?

NAOMI (SYMBOL OF AN UNCERTAIN FUTURE)

By the time she had lost her husband and sons, Naomi was an old woman. All of her safeguards were gone. She didn't even have the luxury of developing a false sense of security. She had lost her husband. She had lost both of her sons—the social security plan of every woman of the ancient world.

Other than the men in their lives, there was no widow's pension. The Moabite nor the Israeli government had Social Security plans. There were no IRAs, no 401(k) plans from which a woman left alone might draw. And although Jewish law protected the widows and orphans: "Do not deprive the alien or the fatherless of justice, or take the cloak of the widow as a pledge" (Deut. 24:17, NIV) and it made sure they were cared for, but this legal provision certainly would not have offered her the kind of life she likely would have had if her husband or sons had lived.

She was concerned about the future of her two daughters-in-law. But, truthfully, can we honestly believe that Naomi really wanted them to leave her to make the journey back to Israel alone? Once, when my mother was in the hospital, I asked my brother if he had planned to visit her. He told me no, because she'd told him it wasn't necessary to come. My response to him was, "And you believed that?"

Whether she really wanted them to go our not, Naomi encouraged the two younger women to return to the land of their mothers because in Oriental countries, the mothers were responsible for the welfare of the daughters. Naomi even issued a Hebrew blessing to her daughters-in-law): "May the LORD show kindness to you, as you have shown to your dead and to me. May the LORD grant that each of you will find rest in the home of another husband" (Ruth 1:8-9, NIV)

Inherent in this story is an indication of the faith of Naomi. She was willing to put the best interests of her daughters-in-law above her own needs. Surely she didn't want to go back to Israel alone. God created us to live in relationship with other human beings. The difficult journey back to Israel surely would have been easier for the old woman if she had some younger companions to accompany her.

Life is full of uncertainties, whether we are young or old, rich or poor. Even those who believe in Jesus Christ find themselves grappling with periods of uncertainty in life. Whether we are young or old, rich or poor, life is full of uncertainties. Even those who believe in Jesus Christ find themselves grappling with periods of uncertainty in life. Everybody lives through a period of an uncertain future. It may even seem at times like you're trapped.

There probably were days when Jesus thought He would never get out of Nazareth. Many students have uncertain days when they think they'll never get out of school. Some days a young mother may think she'll never have a life that doesn't include changing diapers and preparing meals. Some days a young athlete may think he'll never get his chance to show what he's made of. Some days a young singer may think that no one is ever going to recognize her gifts as long as she's singing in church and a few local events. Every person, no matter how successful in life, has gone through some periods of an uncertain future.

Naomi faced an uncertain future because everything she had known, everything that defined her in life, principally being a wife and mother, was gone. She no longer had a reason to stay in Moab so, being an old woman, Naomi longed to be back among the familiar. It's tough to lose your familiar place in life. When you lose your familiar place, you lose your edge in life. You hit a slump.

There are times in all of our lives when we hit a slump—we lose our cutting edge in certain aspects of our lives. At the close of every year, many people are reflecting on things that they need to change in the new year. People start thinking about the areas of their lives—whether physically, spiritually, intellectually, or emotionally—where they've lost their edge and they resolve to get it back.

Some people are in spiritual slumps. They need to get closer to God or they need to restore a broken relationship with God. When you lose your spiritual edge, you don't pray much anymore. You don't praise God for much anymore. You don't thank God anymore for what He's done for you. You can't see the beauty of God in all of creation anymore. You know you're in a slump and you want to go back to the familiar. You want to be taken back, as André Crouch sings, to the place where you first received Him.

Some people are in a physical slump because they've lost their edge. They need to lose a few pounds and have determined to turn over a new leaf in the new year. When you hit a physical slump you lose you edge and your clothes don't fit right anymore. You're not as confident when you stand and walk. You may even start to neglect you're appearance.

Some people are in a mental slump and have lost their intellectual edge. They've become couch potatoes, looking at too much Lifetime Network, BET, or HBO, and not enough CNN or Fox News. They need to enroll in school but have been hanging out at "the club" instead. When you lose your mental edge, your brain becomes like mashed potatoes. You become more concerned with who's having an affair than with the important affairs of the world. You tell yourself that you're satisfied with the menial job you have because going back to school or getting the certification you need is just too much trouble.

Some people have hit an emotional slump and long to return to the familiar. They have lost their edge. The relationship that used to make them smile and bring them joy seems to have grown stale. A man looks at his wife and wonders, "What am I still doing here with her?" The woman doesn't smile anymore when she picks up the telephone and hears her husband's voice on the other end. When you hit a relationship slump, you don't do the little extras for your mate. You become suspicious and sarcastic, and generally unloving. You long to be in a better place with someone.

Perhaps because Naomi was in her own slump she felt as though she had nothing to offer her daughters-in-law. After all, they had each lost a husband, but she had lost her husband and both her sons. Still, despite her slump, there must have been something about her faith journey that impacted Ruth to the extent that she was willing to forsake her homeland and the gods of her heritage to follow Naomi and also accept her God.

We never know the impact that our relationship with God may have on others, especially unbelievers. The relationship between Naomi and Ruth is a powerful reminder to us that each day we are a living testimony to the Lord. What kind of testimony have you given lately?

RUTH (SYMBOL OF FAITH AND OPPORTUNITY)

Ruth chose to make a faith decision. Faith decisions usually are not easy. If living in faith were easy, everybody would do it. Faith decisions are often difficult because, even though we say that we're trusting in God, in reality we're still looking at our circumstances in our own power.

Perhaps Ruth was able to take such a bold step because she knew she had nothing to lose. Perhaps things were not so rosy at the place of Ruth's mother. Perhaps Ruth believed that if she honored her commitments as she had seen her mother-in-law do, then perhaps Naomi's God would bless her in so doing.

Certainly, Ruth was committed to Naomi, but Ruth also was sufficiently invested in Naomi's God that she pronounced an oath upon herself, "May the LORD deal with me, be it ever so severely, if anything but death separates you and me" (Ruth 1:17, NIV). The word "Lord" is literally translated "Yahveh", meaning the One Universal Most High God. She recognized Israel's God as the sovereign ruler of the universe.

Ruth did not put first what would have seemed best for her. How many people today demonstrate that level of commitment—to another person, or even to God? The King James Version of Ruth 1:14 uses the term "clave," or "clung" (NIV), to Naomi. It is the same word used in Genesis 2:24 when God said a man should "cleave" (KJV, or unite) to his wife. As Orpah kissed her mother-in-law good-bye, Ruth reinforced her commitment to Naomi.

In this age of shallow commitments and "I-gotta-think-about-me" mentality, Ruth's determination to remain with Naomi is inspiring. Commitment is becoming a lost virtue. Many people don't commit to God or church. Many don't commit to marriage. Many don't commit to home, family, or even jobs. In general today, we find it difficult to commit because "I gotta think about me!"

Some years ago, I needed surgery that required an overnight hospital stay. Although I was an adult, my parents came in from out-of-town. Not only did they both spend the night with me in the hospital, but both of them spent the week with me at my apartment. My mother had even brought along extra clothes in case something went wrong and she had to stay a little longer. When they were convinced that I was able to care for myself again, which took about a week, they decided to go back home. As they were preparing to leave, I thanked them for coming to care for me. My mother's response was not "You're welcome," but "It was my obligation." For her, motherhood had not ended simply because I was an adult and had moved away from home. But what was most interesting to me about my mother's response was not that it revealed her belief about motherhood; it was the tone with which she spoke. When she responded that caring for me was her obligation, she did not say it with a sense of burden or weariness. Her words reflected a mature life posture—to her, that was simply the way life was.

How much better would life be if more people lived under such a strong conviction to their obligations! How many single mothers would receive regular child support payments.

How many marriages would not end in divorce? How many difficult causes would be championed because those who had committed to it believed that it was their obligation to stick with it to the end?

Ruth had no idea what was waiting for her in Israel. We know the outcome of the story, but it might have been quite different. Going to Israel might have meant starvation. It might have brought with it a lifetime of poverty. For Ruth, going to Israel might have meant persecution rooted in prejudice against her because of her heritage.

Because of her faithfulness to Naomi and her uncompromised acceptance of Israel's God, she was blessed to marry a rich, good-looking man. Not only were Ruth and Naomi not poor, they moved to a place of abundance. Naomi's sorrow was turned to joy. Ruth's uncertainty was turn to security. Ruth had faith in Naomi's God so that she put her trust in Him.

The testimony comes to those who choose Israel over Moab. Just like everybody has a Moab, everybody has an Israel. Moab represents the safe place to which we retreat because we cannot bring ourselves to step out on faith. Although Orpah returned to Moab, there was nothing wrong with what she did. Orpah probably remarried, had children, and lived the rest of her days peacefully in the land of Moab. Orpah gets a bad rap. Though there was nothing really wrong with Orpah's decision to do the sensible thing, the true adventure, the testimony of victory came to Ruth, who took a risk and went to Israel.

For us, Israel represents the place we strive to reach. Israel represents the spiritual place that requires our faith to get there. It is that place that Hebrews 11:1 (NIV) addresses: "being sure of what we hope for and certain of what we do not see." Ruth went with Naomi hoping for a better life, but she knew nothing about that place.

We know nothing about the places where God wants to send us, but we know that God will do what is best for us. Life is full of new places—leaving a job, launching a new career or a new ministry, living without a loved one, adjusting to a new marriage, or even allowing a marriage to go where it has not been before. These new "Israels" can seem a bit frightening because there's always the danger that things won't work out.

You can live a good life if you chose to stay in Moab, but you'll live a better life if you step out on faith and journey to Israel. We have no way of knowing where God wants to send us. We have to be willing to go. God's Word has given us many models of faith: Shadrach, Meshach, and Abednego; Daniel in the lion's den; and the model of our Lord and Savior saying, "Thy will, not mine." Because Jesus gave Himself to the Father's will, He is now seated at the right hand of God.

In the television series "Roots, the Next Generation," Alex Haley's grandfather as a young man took a job as a Pullman porter. Haley was trying to earn enough money to return to college at a time when higher education was no more than a pipe dream for a young black man, no matter how intelligent he was. On one particular train run, Haley extended a kindness to a white passenger and his wife. During the course of the trip, Haley got to know the man and Haley explained his circumstances. Haley was at a crossroads, trying to decide whether to go back home and be a sharecropper or go back to college in hope of a better life. The passenger gave Haley a business card and said something polite like, "I'm sure you'll make the right choice. I want to know what you decide to do. Write and let me know."

Haley decided to return to school, despite the financial obstacles and a general lack of support from his family. When

Haley got to the school, he discovered that his tuition and all of his academic expenses for the entire year were paid. The white passenger whose wife Haley aided had sent the money to the college with the stipulation that Haley's tuition be paid only if he showed up. If Haley had never returned to the college, the monies would have been sent back to the passenger, who just happened to be a millionaire!

We never know where God will send us, or to whom. Usually we want to know where God is taking us. But that's not the most important thing for us to know. The only real question is, when He sends us somewhere or to someone, Will I go, or will I 'play it safe'? Will I trust God, or will I rely on my own common sense? Some people are that way about their salvation; they want to rely on their own faculties to get them through life. Their common sense tells them there is no life after death. Their common sense tells them that God is a pie-in-the-sky notion for fools. But there comes a time when Jesus asks all of us as He asked the Twelve: "Who do you say that I am?" Who is He to you? What will you say when He calls on you?

The prophet Isaiah says "I heard the voice of the Lord saying, 'Whom shall I send? And who will go for us?' And I said, 'Here am I. Send me!'" (Isa 6:8, NIV). Will you go when He calls you? Will you "step up to the plate"? Or will you make a choice for what seems safe and familiar, and perhaps miss the greatest blessing of your life?

DARE TO TAKE SOME RISKS
Questions

1. Why do the things God sometimes calls us to do go against what seems reasonable and practical to the human mind?

2. What were the circumstances during ancient days that made it so difficult for women to be risk takers? Is it equally as difficult for women to be risk takers today? Why or why not?

3. What are some of the positive spiritual aspects of choosing to stay in a place that seems secure? What are some of the negative spiritual aspects of choosing to stay in a place that seems secure?

4. Think of a time when you were like Orpah, choosing security over a faithful risk. Have you ever regretted the decision? Explain your response.

5. Do you find it difficult to think of the best interests of others when you are in an uncertain place, as Naomi was? Or are you reluctant to draw someone you love into your place of uncertainty?

6. What is the best posture for a Christian to have when faced with an uncertain future?

7. Recall a time in your life when things seemed as though they would never change. What did you do to keep an encouraged heart and to keep your eyes looking toward a positive future, no matter how uncertain things seemed at the time?

8. What Scripture passages would you recommend to someone who is in a form of slump, whether physical, spiritual, mental, or emotional?

9. Why are human beings more likely to take a risk when they feel as though they have nothing to lose?

10. Have you ever chosen Moab over Israel? What is your Israel—the place you are longing to reach? What do you think prevents you from getting there?

11. What is your greatest testimony about the power of God moving in your life? Did that testimony come from a calm, secure experience, or was it wrought from faith struggle?

12. Have you reached a point of spiritual development where you trust God to lead you safely no matter where He takes you? If you have, what caused you to get to that point? If not, what do you believe holds you back from trusting God completely?

ABOUT THE AUTHOR
Olivia M. Cloud

OLIVIA M. CLOUD has devoted nearly a quarter century to the field of publishing as a writer, editor, and curriculum developer, primarily in the Christian arena.

An ordained Baptist minister, the author served for ten years as black church editorial and product development coordinator at the Sunday School Board of the Southern Baptist Convention, now LifeWay Christian Resources.

Rev. Cloud now serves as associate editor of curriculum at the R.H. Boyd Publishing Corporation. She is also owner of her own company, which provides editorial and desktop publishing services to a variety of independent authors as well as international publishers, including LifeWay Christian Resources, Focus on the Family, Urban Ministries, Inc., Thomas Nelson Publishers, Cook Communications, HarperCollins, and Judson Press.

An accomplished author, she has published eight books, including *Black Baptist Sunday School Growth* (Convention Press, 1991), *Rules of the Road: A Guide to Spiritual Growth* (National Baptist Publishing Board, 1999), *Life Challenges for Teens* (Boyd Publications, 1999), *Bible Q & A for Kids* (MEGA Corporation, 2000), and *Testify! Testimonies of the Faithful* (MEGA Corporation, 2000). She also has served as a contributing writer to numerous other books, as well as magazines and newspaper articles.

Rev. Cloud serves as associate minister and Christian education ministry chair at Berean Baptist Church in Nashville. Previously, she was assistant pastor of Simeon Baptist Church in Antioch, Tennessee. She is a member of the Committee on Uniform Series of the National Council of Churches, which is responsible for providing Sunday school outlines for Christian publishing providing materials worldwide. Additionally, she is a member of the Committee on Black Congregational Ministries, which is also affiliated with the National Council of Churches.

Rev. Cloud is a graduate of the University of Kentucky, Lexington, and The Southern Baptist Theological Seminary in Louisville, Kentucky.

www.ingramcontent.com/pod-product-compliance
Lightning Source LLC
Chambersburg PA
CBHW032001040426
42448CB00006B/450